MW01137715

walt
whitman

selected poems

SWEET
WATER
PRESS

walt whitman
selected poems

Copyright © 2006 by Sweetwater Press

Produced by Cliff Road Books

ISBN: 1-58173-502-2
ISBN-13: 978-1-58173-502-4

Design by Pat Covert

Printed in China

Table of Contents

walt
whitman

selected poems

In Cabin'd Ships at Sea

In cabin'd ships at sea,
The boundless blue on every side expanding,
With whistling winds and music of the waves—the
        large imperious waves—
Or some lone bark buoy'd on the dense marine,
Where joyous full of faith, spreading white sails,
She cleaves the ether mid the sparkle and the foam
        of day, or under many a star at night,
By sailors young and old haply will I, a
        reminiscence of the land, be read,
In full rapport at last.

Here are our thoughts, voyagers' thoughts,
Here not the land, firm land, alone appears, may then
        by them be said;
The sky o'erarches here, we feel the undulating deck
        beneath our feet,
We feel the long pulsation, ebb and flow of endless
        motion,
The tones of unseen mystery, the vague and vast
        suggestions of the briny world, the liquid-
        flowing syllables,
The perfume, the faint creaking of the cordage, the
        melancholy rhythm,
The boundless vista, and the horizon far and dim, are
        all here,
And this is ocean's poem.

Then falter not O book, fulfil your destiny,
You not a reminiscence of the land alone,
You too as a lone bark cleaving the ether, purpos'd
        I know not whither, yet ever full of faith,
Consort to every ship that sails, sail you!
Bear forth to them folded my love, (dear mariners,
        for you I fold it here, in every leaf;)
Speed on my book! spread your white sails my
        little bark athwart the imperious waves,
Chant on, sail on, bear o'er the boundless blue
        from me to every sea,
This song for mariners and all their ships.

When I Read the Book

When I read the book, the biography famous,
And is this then, (said I) what the author calls a
        man's life?
And so will some one when I am dead and gone
        write my life?
(As if any man really knew aught of my life;
Why even I myself I often think know little or
        nothing of my real life;
Only a few hints, a few diffused faint clews and
        indirections,
I seek for my own use to trace out here.)

Beginning My Studies

Beginning my studies the first step pleas'd me so
much,
The mere fact consciousness, these forms, the
power of motion,
The least insect or animal, the senses, eyesight, love,
The first step I say, awed me and pleas'd me so
much,
I have hardly gone and hardly wish'd to go any
farther,
But stop and loiter all the time to sing it in ecstatic
songs.

I Hear America Singing

I hear America singing, the varied carols I hear,
Those of mechanics, each one singing his as it
      should be blithe and strong,
The carpenter singing his as he measures his plank
      or beam,
The mason singing his as he makes ready for
      work, or leaves off work,
The boatman singing what belongs to him in his
      boat, the deckhand singing on the
      steamboat deck;
The shoemaker singing as he sits on his bench, the
      hatter singing as he stands;
The wood-cutter's song, the ploughboy's on his
      way in the morning, or at noon
      intermission or at sundown,
The delicious singing of the mother, or of the
      young wife at work, or of the girl sewing
      or washing,
Each singing what belongs to him or her and to
      none else,
The day what belongs to the day—at night, the
      party of young fellows, robust, friendly,
Singing, with open mouths, their strong melodious
      songs.

Poets to Come

Poets to come! orators, singers, musicians to
        come!
Not to-day is to justify me and answer what I am
        for,
But you, a new brood, native, athletic, continental,
        greater than before known,
Arouse! for you must justify me.

I myself but write one or two indicative words for
        the future,
I but advance a moment, only to wheel and hurry
        back in the darkness.

I am a man who, sauntering along without fully
        stopping, turns a casual look upon you
        and then averts his face,
Leaving it to you to prove and define it,
Expecting the main things from you.

To the Garden the World

To the garden the world anew ascending,
Potent mates, daughters, sons, preluding,
The love, the life of their bodies, meaning and being,
Curious here behold my resurrection after slumber,
The revolving cycles in their wide sweep having
      brought me again,
Amorous, mature, all beautiful to me, all wondrous,
My limbs and the quivering fire that ever plays
      through them, for reasons, most
      wondrous,
Existing I peer and penetrate still,
Content with the present, content with the past,
By my side or back of me Eve following,
Or in front, and I following her just the same.

From Pent-up Aching Rivers

From pent-up, aching rivers,
From that of myself without which I were nothing,
From what I am determin'd to make illustrious,
        even if I stand sole among men,
From my own voice resonant, singing the phallus,
Singing the song of procreation,
Singing the need of superb children and therein
        superb grown people,
Singing the muscular urge and the blending,
Singing the bedfellow's song, (O resistless yearning!
O for any and each, the body correlative attracting!
O for you whoever you are your correlative body!
        O it, more than all else, you delighting!)
From the hungry gnaw that eats me night and day,
From native moments, from bashful pains, singing
        them,
Seeking something yet unfound, though I have
        diligently sought it many a long year;
Singing the true song of the soul fitful at random,
Renascent with grossest Nature or among animals,
Of that, of them and what goes with them my
        poems informing,
Of the smell of apples and lemons, of the pairing
        of birds,
Of the wet of woods, of the lapping of waves,
Of the mad pushes of waves upon the land, I them
        chanting,

The overture lightly sounding, the strain
        anticipating;
The welcome nearness, the sight of the perfect body,
The swimmer swimming naked in the bath, or
        motionless on his back lying and floating,
The female form approaching, I, pensive, love-
        flesh tremulous aching,
The divine list for myself or you or for any one
        making,
The face, the limbs, the index from head to foot,
        and what it arouses,
The mystic deliria, the madness amorous, the utter
        abandonment,
(Hark close, and still what I now whisper to you,
I love you, O you entirely possess me,
O that you and I escape from the rest and go
        utterly off, free and lawless,
Two hawks in the air, two fishes swimming in the
        sea not more lawless than we;)
The furious storm through me careering, I
        passionately trembling.
The oath of the inseparableness of two together, of
        the woman that loves me, and whom I
        love more than my life, that oath swearing;
(O I willingly stake all for you!
O let me be lost, if it must be so!
O you and I! what is it to us what the rest do or
        think?

What is all else to us? only that we enjoy each
    other and exhaust each other if it must
    be so:)
From the master, the pilot I yield the vessel to,
The general commanding me, commanding all,
    from him permission taking,
From time the programme hastening, (I have
    loiter'd too long, as it is.)
From sex, from the warp and from the woof,
From privacy, from frequent repinings alone,
From plenty of persons near and yet the right
    person not near;
From the soft sliding of hands over me and
    thrusting of fingers through my hair and
    beard,
From the long sustain'd kiss upon the mouth or
    bosom,
From the close pressure that makes me or any man
    drunk, fainting with excess,
From what the divine husband knows, from the
    work of fatherhood,
From exultation, victory, and relief, from the
    bedfellow's embrace in the night,
From the act-poems of eyes, hands, hips and
    bosoms,
From the cling of the trembling arm,
From the bending curve and the clinch,
From side by side the pliant coverlet off-throwing,
From the one so unwilling to have me leave, and
    me just as unwilling to leave,

(Yet a moment, O tender waiter, and I return,)
From the hour of shining stars and dropping dews,
From the night, a moment I emerging flitting out,
Celebrate you act divine and you children
          prepared for,
And you stalwart loins.

I Sing the Body Electric

1

I sing the body electric,
The armies of those I love engirth me and I engirth
        them,
They will not let me off till I go with them,
        respond to them,
And discorrupt them, and charge them full with
        the charge of the soul.

Was it doubted that those who corrupt their own
        bodies conceal themselves?
And if those who defile the living are as bad as
        they who defile the dead?
And if the body does not do as much as the soul?
And if the body were not the soul, what is the
        soul?

2

The love of the body of man or woman balks
        account, the body itself balks account;
That of the male is perfect, and that of the female
        is perfect.

The expression of the face balks account,
But the expression of a well-made man appears not
        only in his face,
It is in his limbs and joints also, it is curiously in
        the joints of his hips and wrists,

It is in his walk, the carriage of his neck, the flex
	of his waist and knees, dress does not hide
	him,
The strong sweet quality he has strikes through the
	cotton and broadcloth,
To see him pass conveys as much as the best
	poem, perhaps more,
You linger to see his back, and the back of his
	neck and shoulder-side.

The sprawl and fulness of babes, the bosoms and
	heads of women, the folds of their dress,
	their style as we pass in the street, the
	contour of their shape downwards,
The swimmer naked in the swimming-bath, seen
	as he swims through the transparent
	green-shine, or lies with his face up and
	rolls silently to and fro in the heave of the
	water,
The bending forward and backward of rowers in
	row-boats, the horseman in his saddle,
Girls, mothers, house-keepers, in all their
	performances,
The group of laborers seated at noon-time with
	their open dinner-kettles, and their wives
	waiting,
The female soothing a child, the farmer's daughter
	in the garden or cow-yard,
The young fellow hoeing corn, the sleigh-driver
	driving his six horses through the crowd,

The wrestle of wrestlers, two apprentice-boys,
　　　quite grown, lusty, good-natured, native-
　　　born, out on the vacant lot at sundown,
　　　after work,
The coats and caps thrown down, the embrace of
　　　love and resistance,
The upper-hold and under-hold, the hair rumpled
　　　over and blinding the eyes;
The march of firemen in their own costumes, the
　　　play of masculine muscle through clean-
　　　setting trowsers and waist-straps,
The slow return from the fire, the pause when the
　　　bell strikes suddenly again, and the
　　　listening on the alert,
The natural, perfect, varied attitudes, the bent
　　　head, the curv'd neck and the counting;
Such-like I love—I loosen myself, pass freely, am
　　　at the mother's breast with the little child,
Swim with the swimmers, wrestle with wrestlers,
　　　march in line with the firemen, and pause,
　　　listen, and count.

3

I know a man, a common farmer, the father of five
　　　sons,
And in them the fathers of sons, and in them the
　　　fathers of sons.

This man was of wonderful vigor, calmness, beauty
　　　of person,

The shape of his head, the pale yellow and white
                of his hair and beard, and the
                immeasurable meaning of his black eyes,
                the richness and breadth of his manners,
These I used to go and visit him to see, he was
                wise also,
He was six feet tall, he was over eighty years old,
                his sons were massive, clean, bearded, tan-
                faced, handsome,
They and his daughters loved him, all who saw
                him loved him,
They did not love him by allowance, they loved
                him with personal love,
He drank water only, the blood show'd like scarlet
                through the clear-brown skin of his face,
He was a frequent gunner and fisher, he sail'd his
                boat himself, he had a fine one presented
                to him by a ship-joiner, he had fowling-
                pieces presented to him by men that loved
                him,
When he went with his five sons and many grand-
                sons to hunt or fish, you would pick him
                out as the most beautiful and vigorous of
                the gang.
You would wish long and long to be with him, you
                would wish to sit by him in the boat that
                you and he might touch each other.

I have perceiv'd that to be with those I like is
enough,
To stop in company with the rest at evening is
enough,
To be surrounded by beautiful, curious, breathing,
laughing flesh is enough,
To pass among them or touch any one or rest my
arm ever so lightly round his or her neck
for a moment, what is this, then?
I do not ask any more delight, I swim in it as in a
sea.

There is something in staying close to men and
women and looking on them, and in the
contact and odor of them, that pleases the
soul well,
All things please the soul, but these please the soul
well.

5

This is the female form,
A divine nimbus exhales from it from head to foot,
It attracts with fierce undeniable attraction,
I am drawn by its breath as if I were no more than
a helpless vapor, all falls aside but myself
and it,
Books, art, religion, time, the visible and solid
earth, and what was expected of heaven or
fear'd of hell, are now consumed,

Mad filaments, ungovernable shoots play out of it,
      the response likewise ungovernable,
Hair, bosom, hips, bend of legs, negligent falling
      hands, all diffused, mine too diffused,
Ebb stung by the flow and flow stung by the ebb,
      love-flesh swelling and deliciously aching,
Limitless limpid jets of love hot and enormous,
      quivering jelly of love, white-blow and
      delirious juice,
Bridegroom night of love, working surely and
      softly into the prostrate dawn,
Undulating into the willing and yielding day,
Lost in the cleave of the clasping and sweet-flesh'd
      day.

This is the nucleus—after the child is born of
      woman, man is born of woman,
This is the bath of birth—this the merge of small
      and large, and the outlet again.

Be not ashamed women, your privilege encloses
      the rest, and is the exit of the rest,
You are the gates of the body, and you are the gates
      of the soul.

The female contains all qualities and tempers
      them,
She is in her place and moves with perfect balance,
She is all things duly veil'd, she is both passive and
      active,

She is to conceive daughters as well as sons, and
    sons as well as daughters.

As I see my soul reflected in Nature;
As I see through a mist, One with inexpressible
    completeness, sanity, and beauty,
See the bent head, and arms folded over the
    breast, the Female I see.

6

The male is not less the soul nor more, he too is
    in his place,
He too is all qualities, he is action and power,
The flush of the known universe is in him,
Scorn becomes him well, and appetite and
    defiance become him well,
The wildest largest passions, bliss that is utmost,
    sorrow that is utmost become him well,
    pride is for him,
The full-spread pride of man is calming and
    excellent to the soul,
Knowledge becomes him, he likes it always, he
    brings every thing to the test of himself,
Whatever the survey, whatever the sea and the sail
    he strikes soundings at last only here,
(Where else does he strike soundings except here?)

The man's body is sacred and the woman's body is
    sacred;

No matter who it is, it is sacred—is it the meanest
        one in the laborers' gang?
Is it one of the dull-faced immigrants just landed
        on the wharf?
Each belongs here or anywhere just as much as the
        well-off, just as much as you,
Each has his or her place in the procession.

(All is a procession,
The universe is a procession, with measured and
        perfect motion.)

Do you know so much yourself that you call the
        meanest ignorant?
Do you suppose you have a right to a good sight,
        and he or she has no right to a sight?
Do you think matter has cohered together from its
        diffuse float, and the soil is on the surface,
        and water runs and vegetation sprouts,
For you only, and not for him and her?

7

A man's body at auction,
(For before the war I often go to the slave-mart
        and watch the sale,)
I help the auctioneer, the sloven does not half
        know his business.

Gentlemen, look on this wonder,
Whatever the bids of the bidders they cannot be
        high enough for it,

For it the globe lay preparing quintillions of years
        without one animal or plant;
For it the revolving cycles truly and steadily roll'd.

In this head the all-baffling brain,
In it and below it the makings of heroes.

Examine these limbs, red, black, or white, they are
        cunning in tendon and nerve;
They shall be stript that you may see them.

Exquisite senses, life-lit eyes, pluck, volition,
Flakes of breast-muscle, pliant backbone and neck,
        flesh not flabby, good-sized arms and legs,
And wonders within there yet.

Within there runs blood,
The same old blood! the same red-running blood!
There swells and jets a heart, there all passions,
        desires, reachings, aspirations,
(Do you think they are not there because they are
        not express'd in parlors and lecture-
        rooms?)

This is not only one man, this the father of those
        who shall be fathers in their turns,
In him the start of populous states and rich
        republics,
Of him countless immortal lives with countless
        embodiments and enjoyments.

26

How do you know who shall come from the
        offspring of his offspring through the
        centuries?
(Who might you find you have come from
        yourself, if you could trace back through
        the centuries?)

                        8

A woman's body at auction,
She too is not only herself, she is the teeming
        mother of mothers,
She is the bearer of them that shall grow and be
        mates to the mothers.

Have you ever loved the body of a woman?
Have you ever loved the body of a man?
Do you not see that these are exactly the same to
        all in all nations and times all over the
        earth?

If any thing is sacred the human body is sacred,
And the glory and sweet of a man is the token of
        manhood untainted,
And in man or woman a clean, strong, firm-fibred
        body, is more beautiful than the most
        beautiful face.

Have you seen the fool that corrupted his own live
        body? or the fool that corrupted her own
        live body?

For they do not conceal themselves, and cannot
  conceal themselves.

9

O my body! I dare not desert the likes of you in
  other men and women, nor the likes of the
  parts of you,
I believe the likes of you are to stand or fall with
  the likes of the soul, (and that they are the
  soul,)
I believe the likes of you shall stand or fall with
  my poems, and that they are poems,
Man's, woman's, child's, youth's, wife's, husband's,
  mother's, father's, young man's, young
  woman's poems,
Head, neck, hair, ears, drop and tympan of the ears,
Eyes, eye-fringes, iris of the eye, eyebrows, and the
  waking or sleeping of the lids,
Mouth, tongue, lips, teeth, roof of the mouth,
  jaws, and the jaw-hinges,
Nose, nostrils of the nose, and the partition,
Cheeks, temples, forehead, chin, throat, back of
  the neck, neck-slue,
Strong shoulders, manly beard, scapula, hind-
  shoulders, and the ample side-round of
  the chest.
Upper-arm, armpit, elbow-socket, lower-arm, arm-
  sinews, arm-bones,
Wrist and wrist-joints, hand, palm, knuckles,
  thumb, forefinger, finger-joints, finger-nails,

Broad breast-front, curling hair of the breast,
         breast-bone, breast-side,
Ribs, belly, backbone, joints of the backbone,
Hips, hip-sockets, hip-strength, inward and
         outward round, man-balls, man-root,
Strong set of thighs, well carrying the trunk above,
Leg-fibres, knee, knee-pan, upper-leg, under-leg,
Ankles, instep, foot-ball, toes, toe-joints, the heel;
All attitudes, all the shapeliness, all the belongings
         of my or your body, or of any one's body,
         male or female,
The lung-sponges, the stomach-sac, the bowels
         sweet and clean,
The brain in its folds inside the skull-frame,
Sympathies, heart-valves, palate-valves, sexuality,
         maternity,
Womanhood, and all that is a woman, and the
         man that comes from woman,
The womb, the teats, nipples, breast-milk, tears,
         laughter, weeping, love-looks, love-
         perturbations and risings,
The voice, articulation, language, whispering,
         shouting aloud,
Food, drink, pulse, digestion, sweat, sleep,
         walking, swimming,
Poise on the hips, leaping, reclining, embracing,
         arm-curving and tightening,
The continual changes of the flex of the mouth,
         and around the eyes,
The skin, the sun-burnt shade, freckles, hair,

The curious sympathy one feels, when feeling with
the hand the naked meat of the body,
The circling rivers, the breath, and breathing it in
and out,
The beauty of the waist, and thence of the hips,
and thence downward toward the knees,
The thin red jellies within you or within me, the
bones, and the marrow in the bones,
The exquisite realization of health;
O I say, these are not the parts and poems of the
body only, but of the soul,
O I say now these are the soul!

Spontaneous Me

Spontaneous me, Nature,
The loving day, the mounting sun, the friend I am
 happy with,
The arm of my friend hanging idly over my
 shoulder,
The hill-side whiten'd with blossoms of the
 mountain ash,
The same late in autumn, the hues of red, yellow,
 drab, purple, and light and dark green,
The rich coverlet of the grass, animals and birds,
 the private untrimm'd bank, the primitive
 apples, the pebble-stones,
Beautiful dripping fragments, the negligent list of
 one after another as I happen to call them
 to me or think of them,
The real poems, (what we call poems being merely
 pictures,)
The poems of the privacy of the night, and of men
 like me,
This poem drooping shy and unseen that I always
 carry, and that all men carry,
(Know once for all, avow'd on purpose, wherever
 are men like me, are our lusty lurking
 masculine poems,)
Love-thoughts, love-juice, love-odor, love-yielding,
 love-climbers, and the climbing sap,
Arms and hands of love, lips of love, phallic
 thumb of love, breasts of love, bellies
 press'd and glued together with love,

Earth of chaste love, life that is only life after love,
The body of my love, the body of the woman I
       love, the body of the man, the body of the
       earth,
Soft forenoon airs that blow from the south-west,
The hairy wild-bee that murmurs and hankers up
       and down, that gripes the full-grown lady-
       flower, curves upon her with amorous firm
       legs, takes his will of her, and holds
       himself tremulous and tight till he is
       satisfied;
The wet of woods through the early hours,
Two sleepers at night lying close together as they
       sleep, one with an arm slanting down
       across and below the waist of the other,
The smell of apples, aromas from crush'd sage-
       plant, mint, birch-bark,
The boy's longings, the glow and pressure as he
       confides to me what he was dreaming,
The dead leaf whirling its spiral whirl and falling
       still and content to the ground,
The no-form'd stings that sights, people, objects,
       sting me with,
The hubb'd sting of myself, stinging me as much
       as it ever can any one,
The sensitive, orbic, underlapp'd brothers, that
       only privileged feelers may be intimate
       where they are,
The curious roamer the hand roaming all over the
       body, the bashful withdrawing of flesh

where the fingers soothingly pause and
edge themselves,
The limpid liquid within the young man,
The vex'd corrosion so pensive and so painful,
The torment, the irritable tide that will not be at
rest,
The like of the same I feel, the like of the same in
others,
The young man that flushes and flushes, and the
young woman that flushes and flushes,
The young man that wakes deep at night, the hot
hand seeking to repress what would
master him,
The mystic amorous night, the strange half-
welcome pangs, visions, sweats,
The pulse pounding through palms and trembling
encircling fingers, the young man all
color'd, red, ashamed, angry;
The souse upon me of my lover the sea, as I lie
willing and naked,
The merriment of the twin babes that crawl over
the grass in the sun, the mother never
turning her vigilant eyes from them,
The walnut-trunk, the walnut-husks, and the
ripening or ripen'd long-round walnuts,
The continence of vegetables, birds, animals,
The consequent meanness of me should I skulk or
find myself indecent, while birds and
animals never once skulk or find
themselves indecent,

The great chastity of paternity, to match the great
        chastity of maternity,
The oath of procreation I have sworn, my Adamic
        and fresh daughters,
The greed that eats me day and night with hungry
        gnaw, till I saturate what shall produce
        boys to fill my place when I am through,
The wholesome relief, repose, content,
And this bunch, pluck'd at random from myself,
It has done its work—I toss it carelessly to fall
        where it may.

Once I Pass'd Through a Populous City

Once I pass'd through a populous city imprinting
       my brain for future use with its shows,
       architecture, customs, traditions,
Yet now of all that city I remember only a woman I
       casually met there who detain'd me for
       love of me,
Day by day and night by night we were together—
       all else has long been forgotten by me,
I remember I say only that woman who
       passionately clung to me,
Again we wander, we love, we separate again,
Again she holds me by the hand, I must not go,
I see her close beside me with silent lips sad and
       tremulous.

In Paths Untrodden

In paths untrodden,
In the growth by margins of pond-waters,
Escaped from the life that exhibits itself,
From all the standards hitherto publish'd, from the
    pleasures, profits, conformities,
Which too long I was offering to feed my soul;
Clear to me now standards not yet publish'd, clear
    to me that my soul,
That the soul of the man I speak for rejoices in
    comrades,
Here by myself away from the clank of the world,
Tallying and talk'd to here by tongues aromatic,
No longer abash'd, (for in this secluded spot I can
    respond as I would not dare elsewhere,)
Strong upon me the life that does not exhibit itself,
    yet contains all the rest,
Resolv'd to sing no songs to-day but those of
    manly attachment,
Projecting them along that substantial life,
Bequeathing hence types of athletic love,
Afternoon this delicious Ninth-month in my forty-
    first year,
I proceed, for all who are or have been young men,
To tell the secret of my nights and days,
To celebrate the need of comrades.

These I Singing in Spring

These I singing in spring collect for lovers,
(For who but I should understand lovers and all
        their sorrow and joy?
And who but I should be the poet of comrades?)
Collecting I traverse the garden the world, but
        soon I pass the gates,
Now along the pond-side, now wading in a little,
        fearing not the wet,
Now by the post-and-rail fences, where the old
        stones thrown there, pick'd from the fields,
        have accumulated,
(Wild-flowers and vines and weeds come up
        through the stones and partly cover them,
        beyond these I pass,)
Far, far in the forest, or sauntering later in
        summer, before I think where I go,
Solitary, smelling the earthy smell, stopping now
        and then in the silence,
Alone I had thought, yet soon a troop gathers
        around me,
Some walk by my side and some behind, and
        some embrace my arms or neck,
They the spirits of dear friends dead or alive,
        thicker they come, a great crowd, and I in
        the middle,
Collecting, dispensing, singing, there I wander
        with them,
Plucking something for tokens, tossing toward
        whoever is near me,

Here, lilac, with a branch of pine,

Here, out of my pocket, some moss which I pull'd
off a live-oak in Florida as it hung trailing
down,

Here, some pinks and laurel leaves, and a handful
of sage,

And here what I now draw from the water, wading
in the pond-side,

(O here I last saw him that tenderly loves me, and
returns again never to separate from me,

And this, O this shall henceforth be the token of
comrades, this calamus-root shall,

Interchange it youths with each other! let none
render it back!)

And twigs of maple and a bunch of wild orange
and chestnut,

And stems of currants and plum-blows, and the
aromatic cedar,

These I compass'd around by a thick cloud of
spirits,

Wandering, point to or touch as I pass, or throw
them loosely from me,

Indicating to each one what he shall have, giving
something to each;

But what I drew from the water by the pond-side,
that I reserve,

I will give of it, but only to them that love as I
myself am capable of loving.

When I Heard at the Close of the Day

When I heard at the close of the day how my
        name had been receiv'd with plaudits in
        the capitol, still it was not a happy night
        for me that follow'd,
And else, when I carous'd, or when my plans were
        accomplish'd, still I was not happy,
But the day when I rose at dawn from the bed of
        perfect health, refresh'd, singing, inhaling
        the ripe breath of autumn,
When I saw the full moon in the west grow pale
        and disappear in the morning light,
When I wander'd alone over the beach, and
        undressing bathed, laughing with the cool
        waters, and saw the sun rise,
And when I thought how my dear friend my lover
        was on his way coming, O then I was
        happy,
O then each breath tasted sweeter, and all that day
        my food nourish'd me more, and the
        beautiful day pass'd well,
And the next came with equal joy, and with the
        next at evening came my friend,
And that night while all was still I heard the waters
        roll slowly continually up the shores,
I heard the hissing rustle of the liquid and sands as
        directed to me whispering to congratulate
        me,

For the one I love most lay sleeping by me under
       the same cover in the cool night,
In the stillness in the autumn moonbeams his face
       was inclined toward me,
And his arm lay lightly around my breast—and
       that night I was happy.

Roots and Leaves Themselves Alone

Roots and leaves themselves alone are these,
Scents brought to men and women from the wild
      woods and pond-side,
Breast-sorrel and pinks of love, fingers that wind
      around tighter than vines,
Gushes from the throats of birds hid in the foliage
      of trees as the sun is risen,
Breezes of land and love set from living shores to
      you on the living sea, to you, O sailors!
Frost-mellow'd berries, and Third-month twigs
      offer'd fresh to young persons wandering
      out in the fields when the winter breaks
      up,
Love-buds put before you and within you whoever
      you are,
Buds to be unfolded on the old terms,
If you bring the warmth of the sun to them they
      will open and bring form, color, perfume,
      to you,
If you become the aliment and the wet they will
      become flowers, fruits, tall branches and
      trees.

Trickle Drops

Trickle drops! my blue veins leaving!
O drops of me! trickle, slow drops,
Candid from me falling, drip, bleeding drops,
From wounds made to free you whence you were
        prison'd,
From my face, from my forehead and lips,
From my breast, from within where I was
        conceal'd, press forth red drops,
        confession drops,
Stain every page, stain every song I sing, every
        word I say, bloody drops,
Let them know your scarlet heat, let them glisten,
Saturate them with yourself all ashamed and wet,
Glow upon all I have written or shall write,
        bleeding drops,
Let it all be seen in your light, blushing drops.

I Saw in Louisiana a Live-Oak Growing

I saw in Louisiana a live-oak growing,
All alone stood it and the moss hung down from
    the branches,
Without any companion it grew there uttering
    joyous leaves of dark green,
And its look, rude, unbending, lusty, made me
    think of myself,
But I wonder'd how it could utter joyous leaves
    standing alone there without its friend
    near, for I knew I could not,
And I broke off a twig with a certain number of
    leaves upon it, and twined around it a
    little moss,
And brought it away, and I have placed it in sight
    in my room,
It is not needed to remind me as of my own dear
    friends,
(For I believe lately I think of little else than of
    them,)
Yet it remains to me a curious token, it makes me
    think of manly love;
For all that, and though the live-oak glistens there
    in Louisiana solitary in a wide flat space,
Uttering joyous leaves all its life without a friend a
    lover near,
I know very well I could not.

To a Stranger

Passing stranger! you do not know how longingly I
        look upon you,
You must be he I was seeking, or she I was
        seeking, (it comes to me as of a dream,)
I have somewhere surely lived a life of joy with
        you,
All is recall'd as we flit by each other, fluid,
        affectionate, chaste, matured,
You grew up with me, were a boy with me or a girl
        with me,
I ate with you and slept with you, your body has
        become not yours only nor left my body
        mine only,
You give me the pleasure of your eyes, face, flesh,
        as we pass, you take of my beard, breast,
        hands, in return,
I am not to speak to you, I am to think of you
        when I sit alone or wake at night alone,
I am to wait, I do not doubt I am to meet you
        again,
I am to see to it that I do not lose you.

I Hear It Was Charged Against Me

I hear it was charged against me that I sought to
        destroy institutions,
But really I am neither for nor against institutions,
(What indeed have I in common with them? or
        what with the destruction of them?)
Only I will establish in Mannahatta and in every
        city of these States inland and seaboard,
And in the fields and woods, and above every keel
        little or large that dents the water,
Without edifices or rules or trustees or any
        argument,
The institution of the dear love of comrades.

Here the Frailest Leaves of Me

Here the frailest leaves of me and yet my strongest
       lasting,
Here I shade and hide my thoughts, I myself do
       not expose them,
And yet they expose me more than all my other
       poems.

Song of the Open Road

1

Afoot and light-hearted I take to the open road,
Healthy, free, the world before me,
The long brown path before me leading wherever I
    choose.

Henceforth I ask not good-fortune, I myself am
    good-fortune,
Henceforth I whimper no more, postpone no
    more, need nothing,
Done with indoor complaints, libraries, querulous
    criticisms,
Strong and content I travel the open road.

The earth, that is sufficient,
I do not want the constellations any nearer,
I know they are very well where they are,
I know they suffice for those who belong to them.

(Still here I carry my old delicious burdens,
I carry them, men and women, I carry them with
    me wherever I go,
I swear it is impossible for me to get rid of them,
I am fill'd with them, and I will fill them in
    return.)

2

You road I enter upon and look around, I believe
       you are not all that is here,
I believe that much unseen is also here.

Here the profound lesson of reception, nor
       preference nor denial,
The black with his woolly head, the felon, the
       diseas'd, the illiterate person, are not
       denied;
The birth, the hasting after the physician, the
       beggar's tramp, the drunkard's stagger, the
       laughing party of mechanics,
The escaped youth, the rich person's carriage, the
       fop, the eloping couple,
The early market-man, the hearse, the moving of
       furniture into the town, the return back
       from the town,
They pass, I also pass, any thing passes, none can
       be interdicted,
None but are accepted, none but shall be dear to
       me.

3

You air that serves me with breath to speak!
You objects that call from diffusion my meanings
       and give them shape!
You light that wraps me and all things in delicate
       equable showers!
You paths worn in the irregular hollows by the
       roadsides!

I believe you are latent with unseen existences,
    you are so dear to me.

You flagg'd walks of the cities! you strong curbs at
    the edges!
You ferries! you planks and posts of wharves! you
    timber-lined sides! you distant ships!

You rows of houses! you window-pierc'd façades!
    you roofs!
You porches and entrances! you copings and iron
    guards!
You windows whose transparent shells might
    expose so much!
You doors and ascending steps! you arches!
You gray stones of interminable pavements! you
    trodden crossings!
From all that has touch'd you I believe you have
    imparted to yourselves, and now would
    impart the same secretly to me,
From the living and the dead you have peopled
    your impassive surfaces, and the spirits
    thereof would be evident and amicable
    with me.

4

The earth expanding right hand and left hand,
The picture alive, every part in its best light,
The music falling in where it is wanted, and
    stopping where it is not wanted,

The cheerful voice of the public road, the gay fresh
      sentiment of the road.

O highway I travel, do you say to me *Do not leave
      me?*
Do you say *Venture not—if you leave me you are lost?*
Do you say *I am already prepared, I am well-
      beaten and undenied, adhere to me?*

O public road, I say back I am not afraid to leave
      you, yet I love you,
You express me better than I can express myself,
You shall be more to me than my poem.

I think heroic deeds were all conceiv'd in the open
      air, and all free poems also,
I think I could stop here myself and do miracles,
I think whatever I shall meet on the road I shall like,
      and whoever beholds me shall like me,
I think whoever I see must be happy.

5

From this hour I ordain myself loos'd of limits and
      imaginary lines,
Going where I list, my own master total and
      absolute,
Listening to others, considering well what they say,
Pausing, searching, receiving, contemplating,
Gently, but with undeniable will, divesting myself
      of the holds that would hold me.

I inhale great draughts of space,
The east and the west are mine, and the north and
the south are mine.

I am larger, better than I thought,
I did not know I held so much goodness.

All seems beautiful to me,
I can repeat over to men and women You have
done such good to me I would do the
same to you,
I will recruit for myself and you as I go,
I will scatter myself among men and women as I go,
I will toss a new gladness and roughness among
them,
Whoever denies me it shall not trouble me,
Whoever accepts me he or she shall be blessed and
shall bless me.

6

Now if a thousand perfect men were to appear it
would not amaze me,
Now if a thousand beautiful forms of women
appear'd it would not astonish me.

Now I see the secret of the making of the best
persons,
It is to grow in the open air and to eat and sleep
with the earth.

Here a great personal deed has room,
(Such a deed seizes upon the hearts of the whole
       race of men,
Its effusion of strength and will overwhelms law
       and mocks all authority and all argument
       against it.)

Here is the test of wisdom,
Wisdom is not finally tested in schools,
Wisdom cannot be pass'd from one having it to
       another not having it,
Wisdom is of the soul, is not susceptible of proof,
       is its own proof,
Applies to all stages and objects and qualities and
       is content,
Is the certainty of the reality and immortality of
       things, and the excellence of things;
Something there is in the float of the sight of
       things that provokes it out of the soul.

Now I re-examine philosophies and religions,
They may prove well in lecture-rooms, yet not
       prove at all under the spacious clouds and
       along the landscape and flowing currents.

Here is realization,
Here is a man tallied—he realizes here what he has
       in him,
The past, the future, majesty, love—if they are
       vacant of you, you are vacant of them.

Only the kernel of every object nourishes;
Where is he who tears off the husks for you and
      me?
Where is he that undoes stratagems and envelopes
      for you and me?

Here is adhesiveness, it is not previously fashion'd,
      it is apropos;
Do you know what it is as you pass to be loved by
      strangers?
Do you know the talk of those turning eye-balls?

7

Here is the efflux of the soul,
The efflux of the soul comes from within through
      embower'd gates, ever provoking
      questions,
These yearnings why are they? these thoughts in
      the darkness why are they?
Why are there men and women that while they are
      nigh me the sunlight expands my blood?
Why when they leave me do my pennants of joy
      sink flat and lank?
Why are there trees I never walk under but large
      and melodious thoughts descend upon
      me?
(I think they hang there winter and summer on
      those trees and always drop fruit as I pass;)
What is it I interchange so suddenly with
      strangers?

What with some driver as I ride on the seat by his
        side?
What with some fisherman drawing his seine by
        the shore as I walk by and pause?
What gives me to be free to a woman's and man's
        good-will? what gives them to be free to
        mine?

8

The efflux of the soul is happiness, here is
        happiness,
I think it pervades the open air, waiting at all times,
Now it flows unto us, we are rightly charged.

Here rises the fluid and attaching character,
The fluid and attaching character is the freshness
        and sweetness of man and woman,
(The herbs of the morning sprout no fresher and
        sweeter every day out of the roots of
        themselves, than it sprouts fresh and sweet
        continually out of itself.)

Toward the fluid and attaching character exudes
        the sweat of the love of young and old,
From it falls distill'd the charm that mocks beauty
        and attainments,
Toward it heaves the shuddering longing ache of
        contact.

9

Allons! whoever you are come travel with me!
Traveling with me you find what never tires.
The earth never tires,
The earth is rude, silent, incomprehensible at first,
       Nature is rude and incomprehensible at
       first,
Be not discouraged, keep on, there are divine
       things well envelop'd,
I swear to you there are divine things more
       beautiful than words can tell.

Allons! we must not stop here,
However sweet these laid-up stores, however
       convenient this dwelling we cannot remain
       here,
However shelter'd this port and however calm
       these waters we must not anchor here,
However welcome the hospitality that surrounds
       us we are permitted to receive it but a little
       while.

10

Allons! the inducements shall be greater,
We will sail pathless and wild seas,
We will go where winds blow, waves dash, and the
       Yankee clipper speeds by under full sail.

Allons! with power, liberty, the earth, the elements,
Health, defiance, gayety, self-esteem, curiosity;
Allons! from all formules!

From your formules, O bat-eyed and materialistic
        priests.

The stale cadaver blocks up the passage—the
        burial waits no longer.

Allons! yet take warning!
He traveling with me needs the best blood, thews,
        endurance,
None may come to the trial till he or she bring
        courage and health,
Come not here if you have already spent the best
        of yourself,
Only those may come who come in sweet and
        determin'd bodies,
No diseas'd person, no rum-drinker or venereal
        taint is permitted here.

(I and mine do not convince by arguments,
        similes, rhymes,
We convince by our presence.)

                    11
Listen! I will be honest with you,
I do not offer the old smooth prizes, but offer
        rough new prizes,
These are the days that must happen to you:
You shall not heap up what is call'd riches,
You shall scatter with lavish hand all that you earn
        or achieve,

You but arrive at the city to which you were
        destin'd, you hardly settle yourself to
        satisfaction before you are call'd by an
        irresistible call to depart,
You shall be treated to the ironical smiles and
        mockings of those who remain behind you,
What beckonings of love you receive you shall
        only answer with passionate kisses of
        parting,
You shall not allow the hold of those who spread
        their reach'd hands toward you.

12

Allons! after the great Companions, and to belong
        to them!
They too are on the road—they are the swift and
        majestic men—they are the greatest
        women,
Enjoyers of calms of seas and storms of seas,
Sailors of many a ship, walkers of many a mile of
        land,
Habituès of many distant countries, habituès of
        far-distant dwellings,
Trusters of men and women, observers of cities,
        solitary toilers,
Pausers and contemplators of tufts, blossoms,
        shells of the shore,
Dancers at wedding-dances, kissers of brides,
        tender helpers of children, bearers of
        children,

Soldiers of revolts, standers by gaping graves,
lowerers-down of coffins,
Journeyers over consecutive seasons, over the
years, the curious years each emerging
from that which preceded it,
Journeyers as with companions, namely their own
diverse phases,
Forth-steppers from the latent unrealized baby-days,
Journeyers gayly with their own youth, journeyers
with their bearded and well-grain'd
manhood,
Journeyers with their womanhood, ample,
unsurpass'd, content,
Journeyers with their own sublime old age of
manhood or womanhood,
Old age, calm, expanded, broad with the haughty
breadth of the universe,
Old age, flowing free with the delicious near-by
freedom of death.

13

Allons! to that which is endless as it was
beginningless,
To undergo much, tramps of days, rests of nights,
To merge all in the travel they tend to, and the
days and nights they tend to,
Again to merge them in the start of superior
journeys,
To see nothing anywhere but what you may reach
it and pass it,

To conceive no time, however distant, but what
　　　　you may reach it and pass it,
To look up or down no road but it stretches and
　　　　waits for you, however long but it
　　　　stretches and waits for you,
To see no being, not God's or any, but you also go
　　　　thither,
To see no possession but you may possess it,
　　　　enjoying all without labor or purchase,
　　　　abstracting the feast yet not abstracting
　　　　one particle of it,
To take the best of the farmer's farm and the rich
　　　　man's elegant villa, and the chaste blessings
　　　　of the well-married couple, and the fruits of
　　　　orchards and flowers of gardens,
To take to your use out of the compact cities as
　　　　you pass through,
To carry buildings and streets with you afterward
　　　　wherever you go,
To gather the minds of men out of their brains as
　　　　you encounter them, to gather the love out
　　　　of their hearts,
To take your lovers on the road with you, for all
　　　　that you leave them behind you,
To know the universe itself as a road, as many
　　　　roads, as roads for traveling souls.

All parts away for the progress of souls,
All religion, all solid things, arts, governments—all
　　　　that was or is apparent upon this globe or

any globe, falls into niches and corners
before the procession of souls along the
grand roads of the universe.

Of the progress of the souls of men and women
along the grand roads of the universe, all
other progress is the needed emblem and
sustenance.

Forever alive, forever forward,
Stately, solemn, sad, withdrawn, baffled, mad,
turbulent, feeble, dissatisfied,
Desperate, proud, fond, sick, accepted by men,
rejected by men,
They go! they go! I know that they go, but I know
not where they go,
But I know that they go toward the best—toward
something great.

Whoever you are, come forth! or man or woman
come forth!
You must not stay sleeping and dallying there in
the house, though you built it, or though
it has been built for you.

Out of the dark confinement! out from behind the
screen!
It is useless to protest, I know all and expose it.

Behold through you as bad as the rest,
Through the laughter, dancing, dining, supping, of
people,

Inside of dresses and ornaments, inside of those
        wash'd and trimm'd faces,
Behold a secret silent loathing and despair.

No husband, no wife, no friend, trusted to hear
        the confession,
Another self, a duplicate of every one, skulking
        and hiding it goes,
Formless and wordless through the streets of the
        cities, polite and bland in the parlors,
In the cars of railroads, in steamboats, in the
        public assembly,
Home to the houses of men and women, at the
        table, in the bedroom, everywhere,
Smartly attired, countenance smiling, form
        upright, death under the breast-bones, hell
        under the skull-bones,
Under the broadcloth and gloves, under the
        ribbons and artificial flowers,
Keeping fair with the customs, speaking not a
        syllable of itself,
Speaking of any thing else but never of itself.

14

Allons! through struggles and wars!
The goal that was named cannot be countermanded.

Have the past struggles succeeded?
What has succeeded? yourself? your nation? Nature?

Now understand me well—it is provided in the
      essence of things that from any fruition of
      success, no matter what, shall come forth
      something to make a greater struggle
      necessary.

My call is the call of battle, I nourish active rebellion,
He going with me must go well arm'd,
He going with me goes often with spare diet,
      poverty, angry enemies, desertions.

15

Allons! the road is before us!
It is safe—I have tried it—my own feet have tried
      it well—be not detain'd!

Let the paper remain on the desk unwritten, and
      the book on the shelf unopen'd!
Let the tools remain in the workshop! let the
      money remain unearn'd!
Let the school stand! mind not the cry of the
      teacher!
Let the preacher preach in his pulpit! let the
      lawyer plead in the court, and the judge
      expound the law.

Camerado, I give you my hand!
I give you my love more precious than money,
I give you myself before preaching or law;
Will you give me yourself? will you come travel
      with me?
Shall we stick by each other as long as we live?

Crossing Brooklyn Ferry

1

Flood-tide below me! I see you face to face!
Clouds of the west—sun there half an hour high—
      I see you also face to face.

Crowds of men and women attired in the usual
      costumes, how curious you are to me!
On the ferry-boats the hundreds and hundreds
      that cross, returning home, are more
      curious to me than you suppose,
And you that shall cross from shore to shore years
      hence are more to me, and more in my
      meditations, than you might suppose.

2

The impalpable sustenance of me from all things at
      all hours of the day,
The simple, compact, well-joined scheme, myself
      disintegrated, every one disintegrated yet
      part of the scheme,
The similitudes of the past and those of the future,
The glories strung like beads on my smallest sights
      and hearings, on the walk in the street and
      the passage over the river,
The current rushing so swiftly and swimming with
      me far away,
The others that are to follow me, the ties between
      me and them,

The certainty of others, the life, love, sight, hearing
  of others.

Others will enter the gates of the ferry and cross
  from shore to shore,
Others will watch the run of the flood-tide,
Others will see the shipping of Manhattan north
  and west, and the heights of Brooklyn to
  the south and east,
Others will see the islands large and small;
Fifty years hence, others will see them as they
  cross, the sun half an hour high,
A hundred years hence, or ever so many hundred
  years hence, others will see them,
Will enjoy the sunset, the pouring-in of the flood-
  tide, the falling-back to the sea of the ebb-
  tide.

3

It avails not, time nor place—distance avails not,
I am with you, you men and women of a generation,
  or ever so many generations hence,
Just as you feel when you look on the river and
  sky, so I felt,
Just as any of you is one of a living crowd, I was
  one of a crowd,
Just as you are refreshed by the gladness of the
  river and the bright flow, I was refreshed,
Just as you stand and lean on the rail, yet hurry
  with the swift current, I stood yet was
  hurried,

Just as you look on the numberless masts of ships
        and the thick-stemmed pipes of
        steamboats, I looked.

I too many and many a time cross'd the river of old,
Watched the Twelfth-month seagulls, saw them
        high in the air floating with motionless
        wings, oscillating their bodies,
Saw how the glistening yellow lit up parts of their
        bodies and left the rest in strong shadow,
Saw the slow-wheeling circles and the gradual
        edging toward the south,
Saw the reflection of the summer sky in the water,
Had my eyes dazzled by the shimmering track of
        beams,
Look'd at the fine centrifugal spokes of light round
        the the shape of my head in the sunlit
        water,
Look'd on the haze on the hills southward and
        south-westward,
Look'd on the vapor as it flew in fleeces tinged
        with violet,
Look'd toward the lower bay to notice the vessels
        arriving,
Saw their approach, saw aboard those that were
        near me,
Saw the white sails of schooners and sloops, saw
        the ships at anchor,
The sailors at work in the rigging or out astride the
        spars,

The round masts, the swinging motion of the
       hulls, the slender serpentine pennants,
The large and small steamers in motion, the pilots
       in their pilot-houses,
The white wake left by the passage, the quick
       tremulous whirl of the wheels,
The flags of all nations, the falling of them at
       sunset,
The scallop-edged waves in the twilight, the ladled
       cups, the frolicsome crests and glistening,
The stretch afar growing dimmer and dimmer, the
       gray walls of the granite storehouses by
       the docks,
On the river the shadowy group, the big steam-tug
       closely flank'd on each side by the barges,
       the hay-boat, the belated lighter,
On the neighboring shore the fires from the
       foundry chimneys burning high and
       glaringly into the night,
Casting their flicker of black contrasted with wild
       red and yellow light over the tops of
       houses, and down into the clefts of streets.

4

These and all else were to me the same as they are
       to you,
I loved well those cities, loved well the stately and
       rapid river,
The men and women I saw were all near to me,

Others the same—others who look back on me
        because I look'd forward to them,
(The time will come, though I stop here to-day,
        and to-night.)

5

What is it then between us?
What is the count of the scores or hundreds of
        years between us?

Whatever it is, it avails not—distance avails not,
        and place avails not,
I too lived, Brooklyn of ample hills was mine,
I too walk'd the streets of Manhattan island, and
        bathed in the waters around it,
I too felt the curious abrupt questionings stir
        within me,
In the day among crowds of people sometimes
        they came upon me,
In my walks home late at night or as I lay in my
        bed they came upon me,
I too had been struck from the float forever held in
        solution,
I too had receiv'd identity by my body,
That I was I knew was of my body, and what I
        should be I knew I should be of my body.

6

It is not upon you alone the dark patches fall,
The dark threw its patches down upon me also,

The best I had done seem'd to me blank and
        suspicious,
My great thoughts as I supposed them, were they
        not in reality meagre?
Nor is it you alone who know what it is to be evil,
I am he who knew what it was to be evil,
I too knitted the old knot of contrariety,
Blabb'd, blush'd, resented, lied, stole, grudg'd,
Had guile, anger, lust, hot wishes I dared not speak,
Was wayward, vain, greedy, shallow, sly, cowardly,
        malignant,
The wolf, the snake, the hog, not wanting in me,
The cheating look, the frivolous word, the
        adulterous wish, not wanting,
Refusals, hates, postponements, meanness,
        laziness, none of these wanting,
Was one with the rest, the days and haps of the rest,
Was call'd by my nighest name by clear loud
        voices of young men as they saw me
        approaching or passing,
Felt their arms on my neck as I stood, or the
        negligent leaning of their flesh against me
        as I sat,
Saw many I loved in the street or ferry-boat or
        public assembly, yet never told them a word,
Lived the same life with the rest, the same old
        laughing, gnawing, sleeping,
Play'd the part that still looks back on the actor or
        actress,

The same old role, the role that is what we make
      it, as great as we like,
Or as small as we like, or both great and small.

7

Closer yet I approach you,
What thought you have of me now, I had as much
      of you—I laid in my stores in advance,
I consider'd long and seriously of you before you
      were born.

Who was to know what should come home to me?
Who knows but I am enjoying this?
Who knows, for all the distance, but I am as good
      as looking at you now, for all you cannot
      see me?

8

Ah, what can ever be more stately and admirable
      to me than mast-hemm'd Manhattan?
River and sunset and scallop-edg'd waves of flood-
      tide?
The seagulls oscillating their bodies, the hay-boat
      in the twilight, and the belated lighter?
What gods can exceed these that clasp me by the
      hand, and with voices I love call me
      promptly and loudly by my nighest name
      as I approach?
What is more subtle than this which ties me to the
      woman or man that looks in my face?

69

Which fuses me into you now, and pours my
          meaning into you?

We understand then do we not?
What I promis'd without mentioning it, have you
          not accepted?
What the study could not teach—what the
          preaching could not accomplish is
          accomplish'd, is it not?

9

Flow on, river! flow with the flood-tide, and ebb
          with the ebb-tide!
Frolic on, crested and scallop-edg'd waves!
Gorgeous clouds of the sunset! drench with your
          splendor me, or the men and women
          generations after me!
Cross from shore to shore, countless crowds of
          passengers!
Stand up, tall masts of Mannahatta! stand up,
          beautiful hills of Brooklyn!
Throb, baffled and curious brain! throw out
          questions and answers!
Suspend here and everywhere, eternal float of
          solution!
Gaze, loving and thirsting eyes, in the house or
          street or public assembly!
Sound out, voices of young men! loudly and
          musically call me by my nighest name!
Live, old life! play the part that looks back on the
          actor or actress!

70

Play the old role, the role that is great or small
  according as one makes it!
Consider, you who peruse me, whether I may not
  in unknown ways be looking upon you;
Be firm, rail over the river, to support those who
  lean idly, yet haste with the hasting
  current;
Fly on, sea-birds! fly sideways, or wheel in large
  circles high in the air;
Receive the summer sky, you water, and faithfully
  hold it till all downcast eyes have time to
  take it from you!
Diverge, fine spokes of light, from the shape of my
  head, or any one's head, in the sunlit
  water!
Come on, ships from the lower bay! pass up or
  down, white-sailed schooners, sloops,
  lighters!
Flaunt away, flags of all nations! be duly lower'd at
  sunset!
Burn high your fires, foundry chimneys! cast black
  shadows at nightfall! cast red and yellow
  light over the tops of the houses!
Appearances, now or henceforth, indicate what
  you are,
You necessary film, continue to envelop the soul,
About my body for me, and your body for you, be
  hung out divinest aromas,
Thrive, cities—bring your freight, bring your
  shows, ample and sufficient rivers,

Expand, being than which none else is perhaps
        more spiritual,
Keep your places, objects than which none else is
        more lasting.

You have waited, you always wait, you dumb,
        beautiful ministers,
We receive you with free sense at last, and are
        insatiate henceforward,
Not you any more shall be able to foil us, or
        withhold yourselves from us,
We use you, and do not cast you aside—we plant
        you permanently within us,
We fathom you not—we love you—there is
        perfection in you also,
You furnish your parts toward eternity,
Great or small, you furnish your parts toward the
        soul.

Song of the Broad-Axe

1

Weapon shapely, naked, wan,
Head from the mother's bowels drawn,
Wooded flesh and metal bone! limb only one, and
        lip only one!
Gray-blue leaf by red-heat grown! helve produced
        from a little seed sown,
Resting the grass amid and upon,
To be lean'd and to lean on.

Strong shapes and attributes of strong shapes,
        masculine trades, sights and sounds;
Long varied train of an emblem, dabs of music,
Fingers of the organist skipping staccato over the
        keys of the great organ.

2

Welcome are all earth's lands, each for its kind,
Welcome are lands of pine and oak,
Welcome are lands of the lemon and fig,
Welcome are lands of gold,
Welcome are lands of wheat and maize, welcome
        those of the grape,
Welcome are lands of sugar and rice,
Welcome the cotton-lands, welcome those of the
        white potato and sweet potato,
Welcome are mountains, flats, sands, forests,
        prairies,

Welcome the rich borders of rivers, table-lands,
      openings,
Welcome the measureless grazing-lands, welcome
      the teeming soil of orchards, flax, honey,
      hemp;
Welcome just as much the other more hard-faced
      lands,
Lands rich as lands of gold or wheat and fruit lands,
Lands of mines, lands of the manly and rugged ores,
Lands of coal, copper, lead, tin, zinc,
Lands of iron—lands of the make of the axe.

3

The log at the wood-pile, the axe supported by it,
The sylvan hut, the vine over the doorway, the
      space clear'd for a garden,
The irregular tapping of rain down on the leaves,
      after the storm is lull'd,
The wailing and moaning at intervals, the thought
      of the sea,
The thought of ships struck in the storm and put
      on their beam ends, and the cutting away
      of masts,
The sentiment of the huge timbers of old-fashion'd
      houses and barns,
The remember'd print or narrative, the voyage at a
      venture of men, families, goods,
The disembarkation, the founding of a new city,
The voyage of those who sought a New England
      and found it, the outset anywhere,

The settlements of the Arkansas, Colorado, Ottawa,
        Willamette,
The slow progress, the scant fare, the axe, rifle,
        saddle-bags;
The beauty of all adventurous and daring persons,
The beauty of wood-boys and wood-men with
        their clear untrimm'd faces,
The beauty of independence, departure, actions
        that rely on themselves,
The American contempt for statutes and ceremonies,
        the boundless impatience of restraint,
The loose drift of character, the inkling through
        random types, the solidification;
The butcher in the slaughter-house, the hands
        aboard schooners and sloops, the
        raftsman, the pioneer,
Lumbermen in their winter camp, daybreak in the
        woods, stripes of snow on the limbs of
        trees, the occasional snapping,
The glad clear sound of one's own voice, the merry
        song, the natural life of the woods, the
        strong day's work,
The blazing fire at night, the sweet taste of supper,
        the talk, the bed of hemlock boughs, and
        the bear-skin;
The house-builder at work in cities or anywhere,
The preparatory jointing, squaring, sawing,
        mortising,
The hoist-up of beams, the push of them in their
        places, laying them regular,

Setting the studs by their tenons in the mortises
        according as they were prepared,
The blows of mallets and hammers, the attitudes
        of the men, their curv'd limbs,
Bending, standing, astride the beams, driving in
        pins, holding on by posts and braces,
The hook'd arm over the plate, the other arm
        wielding the axe,
The floor-men forcing the planks close to be nail'd,
Their postures bringing their weapons downward
        on the bearers,
The echoes resounding through the vacant building;
The huge storehouse carried up in the city well
        under way,
The six framing-men, two in the middle and two
        at each end, carefully bearing on their
        shoulders a heavy stick for a cross-beam,
The crowded line of masons with trowels in their
        right hands rapidly laying the long side-
        wall, two hundred feet from front to rear,
The flexible rise and fall of backs, the continual
        click of the trowels striking the bricks,
The bricks one after another each laid so
        workmanlike in its place, and set with a
        knock of the trowel-handle,
The piles of materials, the mortar on the mortar-
        boards, and the steady replenishing by the
        hod-men;

Spar-makers in the spar-yard, the swarming row of
        well-grown apprentices,
The swing of their axes on the square-hew'd log,
        shaping it toward the shape of a mast,
The brisk short crackle of the steel driven
        slantingly into the pine,
The butter-color'd chips flying off in great flakes
        and slivers,
The limber motion of brawny young arms and
        hips in easy costumes,
The constructor of wharves, bridges, piers, bulk-
        heads, floats, stays against the sea;
The city fireman, the fire that suddenly bursts
        forth in the close-pack'd square,
The arriving engines, the hoarse shouts, the
        nimble stepping and daring,
The strong command through the fire-trumpets,
        the falling in line, the rise and fall of the
        arms forcing the water,
The slender, spasmic, blue-white jets, the bringing
        to bear of the hooks and ladders, and their
        execution,
The crash and cut away of connecting wood-work,
        or through floors if the fire smoulders
        under them,
The crowd with their lit faces watching, the glare
        and dense shadows;
The forger at his forge-furnace and the user of iron
        after him,

The maker of the axe large and small, and the
 welder and temperer,
The chooser breathing his breath on the cold steel
 and trying the edge with his thumb,
The one who clean-shapes the handle, and sets it
 firmly in the socket;
The shadowy processions of the portraits of the
 past users also,
The primal patient mechanics, the architects and
 engineers,
The far-off Assyrian edifice and Mizra edifice,
The Roman lictors preceding the consuls,
The antique European warrior with his axe in
 combat,
The uplifted arm, the clatter of blows on the
 helmeted head,
The death-howl, the limpsey tumbling body, the
 rush of friend and foe thither,
The siege of revolted lieges determin'd for liberty,
The summons to surrender, the battering at castle
 gates, the truce and parley,
The sack of an old city in its time,
The bursting in of mercenaries and bigots
 tumultuously and disorderly,
Roar, flames, blood, drunkenness, madness,
Goods freely rifled from houses and temples,
 screams of women in the gripe of brigands,
Craft and thievery of camp-followers, men
 running, old persons despairing,
The hell of war, the cruelties of creeds,

The list of all executive deeds and words, just or
        unjust,
The power of personality, just or unjust.

4

Muscle and pluck forever!
What invigorates life invigorates death,
And the dead advance as much as the living
        advance,
And the future is no more uncertain than the
        present,
For the roughness of the earth and of man
        encloses as much as the delicatesse of the
        earth and of man,
And nothing endures but personal qualities.

What do you think endures?
Do you think a great city endures?
Or a teeming manufacturing state? or a prepared
        constitution? or the best built steamships?
Or hotels of granite and iron? or any chef-d'oeuvres
        of engineering, forts, armaments?

Away! These are not to be cherish'd for themselves,
They fill their hour, the dancers dance, the
        musicians play for them,
The show passes, all does well enough of course,
All does very well till one flash of defiance.

A great city is that which has the greatest men and
        women,

If it be a few ragged huts it is still the greatest city
      in the whole world.

5

The place where a great city stands is not the place
      of stretch'd wharves, docks, manufactures,
      deposits of produce merely,
Nor the place of ceaseless salutes of new-comers,
      or the anchor-lifters of the departing,
Nor the place of the tallest and costliest buildings
      or shops selling goods from the rest of the
      earth,
Nor the place of the best libraries and schools, nor
      the place where money is plentiest,
Nor the place of the most numerous population.

Where the city stands with the brawniest breed of
      orators and bards,
Where the city stands that is belov'd by these, and
      loves them in return and understands them,
Where no monuments exist to heroes but in the
      common words and deeds,
Where thrift is in its place, and prudence is in its
      place,
Where the men and women think lightly of the laws,
Where the slave ceases, and the master of slaves
      ceases;
Where the populace rise at once against the never-
      ending audacity of elected persons,

Where fierce men and women pour forth as the
       sea to the whistle of death pours its
       sweeping and unript waves,
Where outside authority enters always after the
       precedence of inside authority,
Where the citizen is always the head and ideal,
       and President, Mayor, Governor and what
       not, are agents for pay,
Where children are taught to be laws to themselves,
       and to depend on themselves,
Where equanimity is illustrated in affairs,
Where speculations on the soul are encouraged,
Where women walk in public processions in the
       streets the same as the men,
Where they enter the public assembly and take
       places the same as the men;
Where the city of the faithfulest friends stands,
Where the city of the cleanliness of the sexes stands,
Where the city of the healthiest fathers stands,
Where the city of the best-bodied mothers stands,
There the great city stands.

6

How beggarly appear arguments before a defiant
       deed!
How the floridness of the materials of cities
       shrivels before a man's or woman's look!

All waits or goes by default till a strong being
       appears;

A strong being is the proof of the race and of the
        ability of the universe,
When he or she appears materials are overaw'd,
The dispute on the soul stops,
The old customs and phrases are confronted,
        turn'd back, or laid away.

What is your money-making now? what can it do
        now?
What is your respectability now?
What are your theology, tuition, society, traditions,
        statute-books, now?
Where are your jibes of being now?
Where are your cavils about the soul now?

7

A sterile landscape covers the ore, there is as good as
        the best, for all the forbidding appearance,
There is the mine, there are the miners;
The forge-furnace is there, the melt is
        accomplish'd, the hammers-men are at
        hand with their tongs and hammers,
What always served, and always serves, is at hand.

Than this nothing has better served, it has served all,
Served the fluent-tongued and subtle-sensed
        Greek, and long ere the Greek,
Served in building the buildings that last longer
        than any,
Served the Hebrew, the Persian, the most ancient
        Hindostanee,

Served the mound-raiser on the Mississippi, served
        those whose relics remain in Central
        America,
Served Albic temples in woods or on plains, with
        unhewn pillars and the druids,
Served the artificial clefts, vast, high, silent, on the
        snow-cover'd hills of Scandinavia,
Served those who time out of mind made on the
        granite walls rough sketches of the sun,
        moon, stars, ships, ocean waves,
Served the paths of the irruptions of the Goths,
        served the pastoral tribes and nomads,
Served the long distant Kelt, served the hardy
        pirates of the Baltic,
Served before any of those the venerable and
        harmless men of Ethiopia,
Served the making of helms for the galleys of
        pleasure and the making of those for war,
Served all great works on land and all great works
        on the sea,
For the mediæval ages and before the mediæval ages,
Served not the living only then as now, but served
        the dead.

8

I see the European headsman,
He stands mask'd, clothed in red, with huge legs
        and strong naked arms,
And leans on a ponderous axe.

(Whom have you slaughter'd lately, European
       headsman?
Whose is that blood upon you so wet and sticky?)
I see the clear sunsets of the martyrs,
I see from the scaffolds the descending ghosts,
Ghosts of dead lords, uncrown'd ladies, impeach'd
       ministers, rejected kings,
Rivals, traitors, poisoners, disgraced chieftains and
       the rest.

I see those who in any land have died for the good
       cause,
The seed is spare, nevertheless the crop shall never
       run out,
(Mind you O foreign kings, O priests, the crop
       shall never run out.)

I see the blood wash'd entirely away from the axe,
Both blade and helve are clean,
They spirt no more the blood of European nobles,
       they clasp no more the necks of queens.

I see the headsman withdraw and become useless,
I see the scaffold untrodden and mouldy, I see no
       longer any axe upon it,
I see the mighty and friendly emblem of the power
       of my own race, the newest, largest race.

9

(America! I do not vaunt my love for you;
I have what I have.)

The axe leaps!
The solid forest gives fluid utterances,
They tumble forth, they rise and form,
Hut, tent, landing, survey,
Flail, plough, pick, crowbar, spade,
Shingle, rail, prop, wainscot, jamb, lath, panel, gable,
Citadel, ceiling, saloon, academy, organ, exhibition-
        house, library,
Cornice, trellis, pilaster, balcony, window, turret,
        porch,
Hoe, rake, pitchfork, pencil, wagon, staff, saw,
        jack-plane, mallet, wedge, rounce,
Chair, tub, hoop, table, wicket, vane, sash, floor,
Work-box, chest, string'd instrument, boat, frame,
        and what not,
Capitols of States, and capitol of the nation of
        States,
Long stately rows in avenues, hospitals for orphans
        or for the poor or sick,
Manhattan steamboats and clippers, taking the
        measure of all seas.

The shapes arise!
Shapes of the using of axes anyhow, and the users
        and all that neighbors them,

Cutters down of wood and haulers of it to the
         Penobscot or Kennebec,
Dwellers in cabins among the Californian mountains
         or by the little lakes, or on the Columbia,
Dwellers south on the banks of the Gila or Rio
         Grande, friendly gatherings, the characters
         and fun,
Dwellers along the St. Lawrence, or north in
         Kanada, or down by the Yellowstone,
         dwellers on coasts and off coasts,
Seal-fishers, whalers, arctic seamen breaking
         passages through the ice.

The shapes arise!
Shapes of factories, arsenals, foundries, markets,
Shapes of the two-threaded tracks of railroads,
Shapes of the sleepers of bridges, vast frameworks,
         girders, arches,
Shapes of the fleets of barges, tows, lake and canal
         craft, river craft.
Ship-yards and dry-docks along the Eastern and
         Western seas, and in many a bay and by-
         place,
The live-oak kelsons, the pine planks, the spars,
         the hackmatack-roots for knees,
The ships themselves on their ways, the tiers of
         scaffolds, the workmen busy outside and
         inside,

The tools lying around, the great auger and little
        auger, the adze, bolt, line, square, gouge,
        and bead-plane.

10

The shapes arise!
The shape measur'd, saw'd, jack'd, join'd, stain'd,
The coffin-shape for the dead to lie within in his
        shroud,
The shape got out in posts, in the bedstead posts,
        in the posts of the bride's bed,
The shape of the little trough, the shape of the
        rockers beneath, the shape of the babe's
        cradle,
The shape of the floor-planks, the floor-planks for
        dancers' feet,
The shape of the planks of the family home, the
        home of the friendly parents and children,
The shape of the roof of the home of the happy
        young man and woman, the roof over the
        well-married young man and woman,
The roof over the supper joyously cook'd by the
        chaste wife, and joyously eaten by the
        chaste husband, content after his day's
        work.

The shapes arise!
The shape of the prisoner's place in the court-
        room, and of him or her seated in the
        place,

The shape of the liquor-bar lean'd against by the
      young rum-drinker and the old rum-
      drinker,
The shape of the shamed and angry stairs, trod by
      sneaking footsteps,
The shape of the sly settee, and the adulterous
      unwholesome couple,
The shape of the gambling-board with its devilish
      winnings and losings,
The shape of the step-ladder for the convicted and
      sentenced murderer, the murderer with
      haggard face and pinion'd arms,
The sheriff at hand with his deputies, the silent and
      white-lipp'd crowd, the dangling of the rope.

The shapes arise!
Shapes of doors giving many exits and entrances,
The door passing the dissever'd friend, flush'd and
      in haste,
The door that admits good news and bad news,
The door whence the son left home confident and
      puff'd up,
The door he enter'd again from a long and
      scandalous absence, diseas'd, broken
      down, without innocence, without means.

11

Her shape arises,
She, less guarded than ever, yet more guarded than
      ever,

The gross and soil'd she moves among do not
        make her gross and soil'd,
She knows the thoughts as she passes, nothing is
        conceal'd from her,
She is none the less considerate or friendly therefor,
She is the best belov'd, it is without exception, she
        has no reason to fear, and she does not fear,
Oaths, quarrels, hiccupp'd songs, smutty
        expressions, are idle to her as she passes,
She is silent, she is possess'd of herself, they do
        not offend her,
She receives them as the laws of Nature receive
        them, she is strong,
She too is a law of Nature—there is no law
        stronger than she is.

12
The main shapes arise!
Shapes of Democrac, total, result of centuries,
Shapes ever projecting other shapes,
Shapes of turbulent manly cities,
Shapes of the friends and home-givers of the
        whole earth,
Shapes bracing the earth and braced with the
        whole earth.

Out of the Cradle Endlessly Rocking

Out of the cradle endlessly rocking,
Out of the mocking-bird's throat, the musical shuttle,
Out of the Ninth-month midnight,
Over the sterile sands and the fields beyond,
   where the child leaving his bed wander'd
   alone, bareheaded, barefoot,
Down from the shower'd halo,
Up from the mystic play of shadows twining and
   twisting as if they were alive,
Out from the patches of briers and blackberries,
From the memories of the bird that chanted to me,
From your memories sad brother, from the fitful
   risings and fallings I heard,
From under that yellow half-moon late-risen and
   swollen as if with tears,
From those beginning notes of yearning and love
   there in the mist,
From the thousand responses of my heart never to
   cease,
From the myriad thence-arous'd words,
From the word stronger and more delicious than
   any,
From such as now they start the scene revisiting,
As a flock, twittering, rising, or overhead passing,
Borne hither, ere all eludes me, hurriedly,
A man, yet by these tears a little boy again,
Throwing myself on the sand, confronting the
   waves,

I, chanter of pains and joys, uniter of here and
        hereafter,
Taking all hints to use them, but swiftly leaping
        beyond them,
A reminiscence sing.

Once Paumanok,
When the lilac-scent was in the air and Fifth-
        month grass was growing,
Up this seashore in some briers,
Two feather'd guests from Alabama, two together,
And their nest, and four light-green eggs spotted
        with brown,
And every day the he-bird to and fro near at hand,
And every day the she-bird crouch'd on her nest,
        silent, with bright eyes,
And every day I, a curious boy, never too close,
        never disturbing them,
Cautiously peering, absorbing, translating.

Shine! shine! shine!
Pour down your warmth, great sun!
While we bask, we two together.

Two together!
Winds blow south, or winds blow north,
Day come white, or night come black,
Home, or rivers and mountains from home,
Singing all time, minding no time,
While we two keep together.

Till of a sudden,
May-be kill'd, unknown to her mate,
One forenoon the she-bird crouched not on the nest,
Nor return'd that afternoon, nor the next,
Nor ever appear'd again.

And thenceforward all summer in the sound of the
        sea,
And at night under the full of the moon in calmer
        weather,
Over the hoarse surging of the sea,
Or flitting from brier to brier by day,
I saw, I heard at intervals the remaining one, the
        he-bird,
The solitary guest from Alabama.

Blow! blow! blow!
Blow up sea-winds along Paumanok's shore;
I wait and I wait till you blow my mate to me.

Yes, when the stars glisten'd,
All night long on the prong of a moss-scallop'd
        stake,
Down almost amid the slapping waves,
Sat the lone singer wonderful causing tears.

He call'd on his mate,
He pour'd forth the meanings which I of all men
        know.

Yes my brother I know,
The rest might not, but I have treasur'd every note,
For more than once dimly down to the beach
        gliding,
Silent, avoiding the moonbeams, blending myself
        with the shadows,
Recalling now the obscure shapes, the echoes, the
        sounds and sights after their sorts,
The white arms out in the breakers tirelessly tossing,
I, with bare feet, a child, the wind wafting my hair,
Listen'd long and long.

Listen'd to keep, to sing, now translating the notes,
Following you my brother.

Soothe! soothe! soothe!
Close on its wave soothes the wave behind,
And again another behind embracing and lapping,
        every one close,
But my love soothes not me, not me.

Low hangs the moon, it rose late,
It is lagging—O I think it is heavy with love, with love.

O madly the sea pushes upon the land,
With love, with love.

O night! do I not see my love fluttering out among the
        breakers?
What is that little black thing I see there in the white?

Loud! loud! loud!
Loud I call to you, my love!

High and clear I shoot my voice over the waves,
Surely you must know who is here, is here,
You must know who I am, my love.

Low-hanging moon!
What is that dusky spot in your brown yellow?
O it is the shape, the shape of my mate!
O moon, do not keep her from me any longer.

Land! land! O land!
Whichever way I turn, O I think you could give
        me my mate back again if you only would,
For I am almost sure I see her dimly whichever way I
        look.

O rising stars!
Perhaps the one I want so much will rise, will rise
        with some of you.

O throat! O trembling throat!
Sound clearer through the atmosphere!
Pierce the woods, the earth,
Somewhere listening to catch you must be the one I want.

Shake out carols!
Solitary here, the night's carols!
Carols of lonesome love! death's carols!

Carols under that lagging, yellow, waning moon!
O under that moon where she droops almost down into
             the sea!
O reckless despairing carols.

But soft! sink low!
Soft! let me just murmur,
And do you wait a moment you husky-nois'd sea,
For somewhere I believe I heard my mate responding
             to me,
So faint, I must be still, be still to listen,
But not altogether still, for then she might not come
             immediately to me.

Hither my love!
Here I am! here!
With this just-sustain'd note I announce myself to you,
This gentle call is for you my love, for you.

Do not be decoy'd elsewhere,
That is the whistle of the wind, it is not my voice,
That is the fluttering, the fluttering of the spray,
Those are the shadows of leaves.

O darkness! O in vain!
O I am very sick and sorrowful.

O brown halo in the sky near the moon, drooping upon
             the sea!
O troubled reflection in the sea!

O throat! O throbbing heart!
And I singing uselessly, uselessly all the night.

O past! O happy life! O songs of joy!
In the air, in the woods, over fields,
Loved! loved! loved! loved! loved!
But my mate no more, no more with me!
We two together no more.

The aria sinking,
All else continuing, the stars shining,
The winds blowing, the notes of the bird
        continuous echoing,
With angry moans the fierce old mother
        incessantly moaning,
On the sands of Paumanok's shore gray and rustling,
The yellow half-moon enlarged, sagging down,
        drooping, the face of the sea almost
        touching,
The boy ecstatic, with his bare feet the waves, with
        his hair the atmosphere dallying,
The love in the heart long pent, now loose, now at
        last tumultuously bursting,
The aria's meaning, the ears, the soul, swiftly
        depositing,
The strange tears down the cheeks coursing,
The colloquy there, the trio, each uttering,
The undertone, the savage old mother incessantly
        crying,

To the boy's soul's questions sullenly timing, some
    drown'd secret hissing,
To the outsetting bard.

Demon or bird! (said the boy's soul,)
Is it indeed toward your mate you sing? or is it
    really to me?
For I, that was a child, my tongue's use sleeping,
    now I have heard you,
Now in a moment I know what I am for, I awake,
And already a thousand singers, a thousand songs,
    clearer, louder and more sorrowful than
    yours,
A thousand warbling echoes have started to life
    within me, never to die.

O you singer solitary, singing by yourself,
    projecting me,
O solitary me listening, never more shall I cease
    perpetuating you,
Never more shall I escape, never more the
    reverberations,
Never more the cries of unsatisfied love be absent
    from me,
Never again leave me to be the peaceful child I
    was before what there in the night,
By the sea under the yellow and sagging moon,
The messenger there arous'd, the fire, the sweet
    hell within,
The unknown want, the destiny of me.

O give me the clew! (it lurks in the night here
　　　　somewhere,)
O if I am to have so much, let me have more!

A word then, (for I will conquer it,)
The word final, superior to all,
Subtle, sent up—what is it?—I listen;
Are you whispering it, and have been all the time,
　　　　you sea-waves?
Is that it from your liquid rims and wet sands?

Whereto answering, the sea,
Delaying not, hurrying not,
Whisper'd me through the night, and very plainly
　　　　before daybreak,
Lisp'd to me the low and delicious word death,
And again death, death, death, death,
Hissing melodious, neither like the bird nor like
　　　　my arous'd child's heart,
But edging near as privately for me rustling at my
　　　　feet,
Creeping thence steadily up to my ears and laving
　　　　me softly all over,
Death, death, death, death, death.

Which I do not forget,
But fuse the song of my dusky demon and brother,
That he sang to me in the moonlight on
　　　　Paumanok's gray beach,
With the thousand responsive songs at random,

My own songs awaked from that hour,
And with them the key, the word up from the
      waves,
The word of the sweetest song and all songs,
That strong and delicious word which, creeping to
      my feet,
(Or like some old crone rocking the cradle,
      swathed in sweet garments, bending
      aside,)
The sea whisper'd me.

When I Heard the Learn'd Astronomer

When I heard the learn'd astronomer,
When the proofs, the figures, were ranged in
       columns before me,
When I was shown the charts and diagrams, to
       add, divide, and measure them,
When I sitting heard the astronomer where he
       lectured with much applause in the
       lecture-room,
How soon unaccountable I became tired and sick,
Till rising and gliding out I wander'd off by myself,
In the mystical moist night-air, and from time to
       time,
Look'd up in perfect silence at the stars.

The Dalliance of the Eagles

Skirting the river road, (my forenoon walk, my
      rest,)
Skyward in air a sudden muffled sound, the
      dalliance of the eagles,
The rushing amorous contact high in space
      together,
The clinching interlocking claws, a living, fierce,
      gyrating wheel,
Four beating wings, two beaks, a swirling mass
      tight grappling,
In tumbling, turning clustering loops, straight
      downward falling,
Till o'er the river pois'd, the twain yet one, a
      moment's lull,
A motionless still balance in the air, then parting,
      talons loosing,
Upward again on slow-firm pinions slanting, their
      separate diverse flight,
She hers, he his, pursuing.

Beat! Beat! Drums!

Beat! beat! drums!—blow! bugles! blow!
Through the windows—through doors—burst like
a ruthless force,
Into the solemn church, and scatter the
congregation,
Into the school where the scholar is studying;
Leave not the bridegroom quiet—no happiness
must he have now with his bride,
Nor the peaceful farmer any peace, ploughing his
field or gathering his grain,
So fierce you whirr and pound you drums—so
shrill you bugles blow.

Beat! beat! drums!—blow! bugles! blow!
Over the traffic of cities—over the rumble of
wheels in the streets;
Are beds prepared for sleepers at night in the
houses? no sleepers must sleep in those
beds,
No bargainers' bargains by day—no brokers or
speculators—would they continue?
Would the talkers be talking? would the singer
attempt to sing?
Would the lawyer rise in the court to state his case
before the judge?
Then rattle quicker, heavier drums—you bugles
wilder blow.

Beat! beat! drums!—blow! bugles! blow!
Make no parley—stop for no expostulation,
Mind not the timid—mind not the weeper or
       prayer,
Mind not the old man beseeching the young man,
Let not the child's voice be heard, nor the mother's
       entreaties,
Make even the trestles to shake the dead where
       they lie awaiting the hearses,
So strong you thump O terrible drums—so loud
       you bugles blow.

Calvary Crossing a Ford

A line in long array where they wind betwixt
      green islands,
They take a serpentine course, their arms flash in
      the sun—hark to the musical clank,
Behold the silvery river, in it the splashing horses
      loitering stop to drink,
Behold the brown-faced men, each group, each
      person a picture, the negligent rest on the
      saddles,
Some emerge on the opposite bank, others are just
      entering the ford—while,
Scarlet and blue and snowy white,
The guidon flags flutter gayly in the wind.

Come Up From the Fields Father

Come up from the fields father, here's a letter from
        our Pete,
And come to the front door mother, here's a letter
        from thy dear son.

Lo, 'tis autumn,
Lo, where the trees, deeper green, yellower and
        redder,
Cool and sweeten Ohio's villages with leaves
        fluttering in the moderate wind,
Where apples ripe in the orchards hang and grapes
        on the trellis'd vines,
(Smell you the smell of the grapes on the vines?
Smell you the buckwheat where the bees were
        lately buzzing?)
Above all, lo, the sky so calm, so transparent after
        the rain, and with wondrous clouds,
Below too, all calm, all vital and beautiful, and the
        farm prospers well.

Down in the fields all prospers well,
But now from the fields come father, come at the
        daughter's call,
And come to the entry mother, to the front door
        come right away.

Fast as she can she hurries, something ominous,
        her steps trembling,

She does not tarry to smooth her hair nor adjust
      her cap.

Open the envelope quickly,
O this is not our son's writing, yet his name is sign'd,
O a strange hand writes for our dear son, O
      stricken mother's soul!
All swims before her eyes, flashes with black, she
      catches the main words only,
Sentences broken, *gunshot wound in the breast,*
      cavalry skirmish, taken to hospital,
At present low, but will soon be better.

Ah now the single figure to me,
Amid all teeming and wealthy Ohio with all its
      cities and farms,
Sickly white in the face and dull in the head, very
      faint,
By the jamb of a door leans.

Grieve not so, dear mother, (the just-grown daughter
      speaks through her sobs,
The little sisters huddle around speechless and
      dismay'd,)
See, dearest mother, the letter says Pete will soon be
      better.

Alas poor boy, he will never be better, (nor maybe
      needs to be better, that brave and simple
      soul,)

While they stand at home at the door he is dead
    already,
The only son is dead.

But the mother needs to be better,
She with thin form presently drest in black,
By day her meals untouch'd, then at night fitfully
    sleeping, often waking,
In the midnight waking, weeping, longing with
    one deep longing,
O that she might withdraw unnoticed, silent from
    life escape and withdraw,
To follow, to seek, to be with her dear dead son.

Vigil Strange I Kept on the Field One Night

Vigil strange I kept on the field one night;
When you my son and my comrade dropt at my
    side that day,
One look I but gave which your dear eyes return'd
    with a look I shall never forget,
One touch of your hand to mine O boy, reach'd up
    as you lay on the ground,
Then onward I sped in the battle, the even-
    contested battle,
Till late in the night reliev'd to the place at last
    again I made my way,
Found you in death so cold dear comrade, found
    your body son of responding kisses, (never
    again on earth responding,)
Bared your face in the starlight, curious the scene,
    cool blew the moderate night-wind,
Long there and then in vigil I stood, dimly around
    me the battle-field spreading,
Vigil wondrous and vigil sweet there in the
    fragrant silent night,
But not a tear fell, not even a long-drawn sigh,
    long, long I gazed,
Then on the earth partially reclining sat by your
    side leaning my chin in my hands,
Passing sweet hours, immortal and mystic hours
    with you dearest comrade—not a tear, not
    a word,

Vigil of silence, love and death, vigil for you my
son and my soldier,
As onward silently stars aloft, eastward new ones
upward stole,
Vigil final for you brave boy, (I could not save you,
swift was your death,
I faithfully loved you and cared for you living, I
think we shall surely meet again,)
Till at latest lingering of the night, indeed just as
the dawn appear'd,
My comrade I wrapt in his blanket, envelop'd well
his form,
Folded the blanket well, tucking it carefully over
head and carefully under feet,
And there and then and bathed by the rising sun,
my son in his grave, in his rude-dug grave
I deposited,
Ending my vigil strange with that, vigil of night
and battle-field dim,
Vigil for boy of responding kisses, (never again on
earth responding,)
Vigil for comrade swiftly slain, vigil I never forget,
how as day brighten'd,
I rose from the chill ground and folded my soldier
well in his blanket,
And buried him where he fell.

A March in the Ranks Hard-Prest, And the Road Unknown

A march in the ranks hard-prest, and the road
        unknown,
A route through a heavy wood with muffled steps
        in the darkness,
Our army foil'd with loss severe, and the sullen
        remnant retreating,
Till after midnight glimmer upon us the lights of a
        dim-lighted building,
We come to an open space in the woods, and halt
        by the dim-lighted building,
'Tis a large old church at the crossing roads, now
        an impromptu hospital,
Entering but for a minute I see a sight beyond all
        the pictures and poems ever made,
Shadows of deepest, deepest black, just lit by
        moving candles and lamps,
And by one great pitchy torch stationary with wild
        red flame and clouds of smoke,
By these, crowds, groups of forms vaguely I see on
        the floor, some in the pews laid down,
At my feet more distinctly a soldier, a mere lad, in
        danger of bleeding to death, (he is shot in
        the abdomen,)
I stanch the blood temporarily, (the youngster's
        face is white as a lily,)
Then before I depart I sweep my eyes o'er the
        scene fain to absorb it all,

Faces, varieties, postures beyond description, most
        in obscurity, some of them dead,
Surgeons operating, attendants holding lights, the
        smell of ether, the odor of blood,
The crowd, O the crowd of the bloody forms, the
        yard outside also fill'd,
Some on the bare ground, some on planks or
        stretchers, some in the death-spasm
        sweating,
An occasional scream or cry, the doctor's shouted
        orders or calls,
The glisten of the little steel instruments catching
        the glint of the torches,
These I resume as I chant, I see again the forms, I
        smell the odor,
Then hear outside the orders given, *Fall in, my
        men, fall in;*
But first I bend to the dying lad, his eyes open, a
        half-smile gives he me,
Then the eyes close, calmly close, and I speed
        forth to the darkness,
Resuming, marching, ever in darkness marching,
        on in the ranks,
The unknown road still marching.

The Wound-Dresser

1

An old man bending I come among new faces,
Years looking backward resuming in answer to
      children,
Come tell us old man, as from young men and
      maidens that love me,
(Arous'd and angry, I'd thought to beat the alarum,
      and urge relentless war,
But soon my fingers failed me, my face droop'd
      and I resign'd myself,
To sit by the wounded and soothe them, or silently
      watch the dead;)
Years hence of these scenes, of these furious
      passions, these chances,
Of unsurpass'd heroes, (was one side so brave? the
      other was equally brave;)
Now be witness again, paint the mightiest armies
      of earth,
Of those armies so rapid so wondrous what saw
      you to tell us?
What stays with you latest and deepest? of curious
      panics,
Of hard-fought engagements or sieges tremendous
      what deepest remains?

2

O maidens and young men I love and that love me,
What you ask of my days those the strangest and
      sudden your talking recalls,

Soldier alert I arrive after a long march cover'd
      with sweat and dust,
In the nick of time I come, plunge in the fight,
      loudly shout in the rush of successful
      charge,
Enter the captur'd works—yet lo, like a swift-
      running river they fade,
Pass and are gone they fade—I dwell not on
      soldiers' perils or soldiers' joys,
(Both I remember well—many the hardships, few
      the joys, yet I was content.)

But in silence, in dreams' projections,
While the world of gain and appearance and mirth
      goes on,
So soon what is over forgotten, and waves wash
      the imprints off the sand,
With hinged knees returning I enter the doors,
      (while for you up there,
Whoever you are, follow without noise and be of
      strong heart.)

Bearing the bandages, water and sponge,
Straight and swift to my wounded I go,
Where they lie on the ground after the battle
      brought in,
Where their priceless blood reddens the grass the
      ground,
Or to the rows of the hospital tent, or under the
      roof'd hospital,

To the long rows of cots up and down each side I
return,
To each and all one after another I draw near, not
one do I miss,
An attendant follows holding a tray, he carries a
refuse pail,
Soon to be fill'd with clotted rags and blood,
emptied, and fill'd again.

I onward go, I stop,
With hinged knees and steady hand to dress
wounds,
I am firm with each, the pangs are sharp yet
unavoidable,
One turns to me his appealing eyes—poor boy! I
never knew you,
Yet I think I could not refuse this moment to die
for you, if that would save you.

3

On, on I go, (open doors of time! open hospital
doors!)
The crush'd head I dress, (poor crazed hand tear
not the bandage away,)
The neck of the cavalry-man with the bullet
through and through I examine,
Hard the breathing rattles, quite glazed already the
eye, yet life struggles hard,
(Come sweet death! be persuaded O beautiful death!
In mercy come quickly.)

From the stump of the arm, the amputated hand,
I undo the clotted lint, remove the slough, wash
        off the matter and blood,
Back on his pillow the soldier bends with curv'd
        neck and side-falling head,
His eyes are closed, his face is pale, he dares not
        look on the bloody stump,
And has not yet look'd on it.

I dress a wound in the side, deep, deep,
But a day or two more, for see the frame all wasted
        and sinking,
And the yellow-blue countenance see.

I dress the perforated shoulder, the foot with the
        bullet-wound,
Cleanse the one with a gnawing and putrid
        gangrene, so sickening, so offensive,
While the attendant stands behind aside me
        holding the tray and pail.

I am faithful, I do not give out,
The fractur'd thigh, the knee, the wound in the
        abdomen,
These and more I dress with impassive hand, (yet
        deep in my breast a fire, a burning flame.)

Thus in silence in dreams' projections,
Returning, resuming, I thread my way through the
        hospitals,
The hurt and wounded I pacify with soothing hand,
I sit by the restless all the dark night, some are so
        young,
Some suffer so much, I recall the experience sweet
        and sad,
(Many a soldier's loving arms about this neck have
        cross'd and rested,
Many a soldier's kiss dwells on these bearded lips.)

Give Me the Splendid, Silent Sun

1

Give me the splendid silent sun, with all his beams
full-dazzling,
Give me juicy autumnal fruit ripe and red from the
orchard,
Give me a field where the unmow'd grass grows,
Give me an arbor, give me the trellis'd grape,
Give me fresh corn and wheat, give me serene-
moving animals teaching content,
Give me nights perfectly quiet, as on high plateaus
west of the Mississippi, and I looking up at
the stars,
Give me odorous at sunrise a garden of beautiful
flowers where I can walk undisturb'd,
Give me for marriage a sweet-breath'd woman of
whom I should never tire,
Give me a perfect child, give me away aside from
the noise of the world a rural domestic life,
Give me to warble spontaneous songs recluse by
myself, for my own ears only,
Give me solitude, give me Nature, give me again,
O Nature, your primal sanities!

These demanding to have them, (tired with ceaseless
excitement, and rack'd by the war-strife,)
These to procure, incessantly asking, rising in cries
from my heart,
While yet incessantly asking, still I adhere to my city,

Day upon day and year upon year O city, walking
      your streets,
Where you hold me enchain'd a certain time,
      refusing to give me up,
Yet giving to make me glutted, enrich'd of soul,
      you give me forever faces;
(O I see what I sought to escape, confronting,
      reversing my cries,
I see my own soul trampling down what it ask'd for.)

2

Keep your splendid silent sun,
Keep your woods, O Nature, and the quiet places
      by the woods,
Keep your fields of clover and timothy, and your
      corn-fields and orchards,
Keep the blossoming buckwheat fields where the
      Ninth-month bees hum;
Give me faces and streets—give me these
      phantoms incessant and endless along the
      trottoirs!
Give me interminable eyes—give me women—give
      me comrades and lovers by the thousand!
Let me see new ones every day—let me hold new
      ones by the hand every day!
Give me such shows—give me the streets of
      Manhattan!
Give me Broadway, with the soldiers marching—
      give me the sound of the trumpets and
      drums!

(The soldiers in companies or regiments—some
        starting away, flush'd and reckless,
Some, their time up, returning with thinn'd ranks,
        young, yet very old, worn, marching,
        noticing nothing;)
Give me the shores and the wharves heavy-fringed
        with black ships!
O such for me! O an intense life, full to repletion
        and varied!
The life of the theatre, bar-room, huge hotel, for me!
The saloon of the steamer! the crowded excursion
        for me! the torch-light procession!
The dense brigade bound for the war, with high
        piled military wagons following;
People, endless, streaming, with strong voices,
        passions, pageants,
Manhattan streets with their powerful throbs, with
        beating drums as now,
The endless and noisy chorus, the rustle and clank
        of muskets, (even the sight of the
        wounded,)
Manhattan crowds, with their turbulent musical
        chorus!
Manhattan faces and eyes forever for me.

World Take Good Notice

World take good notice, silver stars fading,
Milky hue ript, weft of white detaching,
Coals thirty-eight, baleful and burning,
Scarlet, significant, hands off warning,
Now and henceforth flaunt from these shores.

Reconciliation

Word over all, beautiful as the sky,
Beautiful that war and all its deeds of carnage must
       in time be utterly lost,
That the hands of the sisters Death and Night
       incessantly softly wash again, and ever
       again, this soil'd world;
For my enemy is dead, a man divine as myself is
       dead,
I look where he lies white-faced and still in the
       coffin—I draw near,
Bend down and touch lightly with my lips the
       white face in the coffin.

As I Lay With My Head in Your Lap Camerado

As I lay with my head in your lap camerado,
The confession I made I resume, what I said to
      you and the open air I resume,
I know I am restless and make others so,
I know my words are weapons full of danger, full
      of death,
For I confront peace, security, and all the settled
      laws, to unsettle them,
I am more resolute because all have denied me
      than I could ever have been had all
      accepted me,
I heed not and have never heeded either
      experience, cautions, majorities, nor
      ridicule,
And the threat of what is call'd hell is little or
      nothing to me,
And the lure of what is call'd heaven is little or
      nothing to me;
Dear camerado! I confess I have urged you onward
      with me, and still urge you, without the
      least idea what is our destination,
Or whether we shall be victorious, or utterly
      quell'd and defeated.

Adieu to a Soldier

Adieu O soldier,
You of the rude campaigning, (which we shared,)
The rapid march, the life of the camp,
The hot contention of opposing fronts, the long
        manoeuvre,
Red battles with their slaughter, the stimulus, the
        strong terrific game,
Spell of all brave and manly hearts, the trains of
        time through you and like of you all fill'd,
With war and war's expression.

Adieu dear comrade,
Your mission is fulfill'd—but I, more warlike,
Myself and this contentious soul of mine,
Still on our own campaigning bound,
Through untried roads with ambushes opponents
        lined,
Through many a sharp defeat and many a crisis,
        often baffled,
Here marching, ever marching on, a war fight
        out—aye here,
To fiercer, weightier battles give expression.

When Lilacs Last in the Dooryard Bloom'd

1

When lilacs last in the dooryard bloom'd,
And the great star early droop'd in the western sky
     in the night,
I mourn'd, and yet shall mourn with ever-
     returning spring.

Ever-returning spring, trinity sure to me you bring,
Lilac blooming perennial and drooping star in the
     west,
And thought of him I love.

2

O powerful western fallen star!
O shades of night—O moody, tearful night!
O great star disappear'd—O the black murk that
     hides the star!
O cruel hands that hold me powerless—O helpless
     soul of me!
O harsh surrounding cloud that will not free my
     soul.

3

In the dooryard fronting an old farm-house near
     the white-wash'd palings,
Stands the lilac-bush tall-growing with heart-
     shaped leaves of rich green,
With many a pointed blossom rising delicate, with
     the perfume strong I love,

With every leaf a miracle—and from this bush in
          the dooryard,
With delicate-color'd blossoms and heart-shaped
          leaves of rich green,
A sprig with its flower I break.

                    4

In the swamp in secluded recesses,
A shy and hidden bird is warbling a song.

Solitary the thrush,
The hermit withdrawn to himself, avoiding the
          settlements,
Sings by himself a song.

Song of the bleeding throat,
Death's outlet song of life, (for well dear brother I
          know,
If thou wast not granted to sing thou would'st
          surely die.)

                    5

Over the breast of the spring, the land, amid cities,
Amid lanes and through old woods, where lately
          the violets peep'd from the ground,
          spotting the gray debris,
Amid the grass in the fields each side of the lanes,
          passing the endless grass,
Passing the yellow-spear'd wheat, every grain from
          its shroud in the dark-brown fields uprisen,

Passing the apple-tree blows of white and pink in
    the orchards,
Carrying a corpse to where it shall rest in the grave,
Night and day journeys a coffin.

6

Coffin that passes through lanes and streets,
Through day and night with the great cloud
    darkening the land,
With the pomp of the inloop'd flags with the cities
    draped in black,
With the show of the States themselves as of
    crape-veil'd women standing,
With processions long and winding and the
    flambeaus of the night,
With the countless torches lit, with the silent sea
    of faces and the unbared heads,
With the waiting depot, the arriving coffin, and the
    sombre faces,
With dirges through the night, with the thousand
    voices rising strong and solemn,
With all the mournful voices of the dirges pour'd
    around the coffin,
The dim-lit churches and the shuddering organs—
    where amid these you journey,
With the tolling tolling bells' perpetual clang,
Here, coffin that slowly passes,
I give you my sprig of lilac.

7

(Nor for you, for one alone,
Blossoms and branches green to coffins all I bring,
For fresh as the morning, thus would I chant a
       song for you O sane and sacred death.

All over bouquets of roses,
O death, I cover you over with roses and early lilies,
But mostly and now the lilac that blooms the first,
Copious I break, I break the sprigs from the bushes,
With loaded arms I come, pouring for you,
For you and the coffins all of you O death.)

8

O western orb sailing the heaven,
Now I know what you must have meant as a
       month since I walk'd,
As I walk'd in silence the transparent shadowy
       night,
As I saw you had something to tell as you bent to
       me night after night,
As you droop'd from the sky low down as if to my
       side, (while the other stars all look'd on,)
As we wander'd together the solemn night, (for
       something I know not what kept me from
       sleep,)
As the night advanced, and I saw on the rim of the
       west how full you were of woe,
As I stood on the rising ground in the breeze in
       the cool transparent night,

As I watch'd where you pass'd and was lost in the
       netherward black of the night,
As my soul in its trouble dissatisfied sank, as
       where you sad orb,
Concluded, dropt in the night, and was gone.

9

Sing on there in the swamp,
O singer bashful and tender, I hear your notes, I
       hear your call,
I hear, I come presently, I understand you,
But a moment I linger, for the lustrous star has
       detain'd me,
The star my departing comrade holds and detains
       me.

10

O how shall I warble myself for the dead one there
       I loved?
And how shall I deck my song for the large sweet
       soul that has gone?
And what shall my perfume be for the grave of
       him I love?

Sea-winds blown from east and west,
Blown from the Eastern sea and blown from the
       Western sea, till there on the prairies
       meeting,
These and with these and the breath of my chant,
I'll perfume the grave of him I love.

11

O what shall I hang on the chamber walls?
And what shall the pictures be that I hang on the
        walls,
To adorn the burial-house of him I love?

Pictures of growing spring and farms and homes,
With the Fourth-month eve at sundown, and the
        gray smoke lucid and bright,
With floods of the yellow gold of the gorgeous,
        indolent, sinking sun, burning, expanding
        the air,
With the fresh sweet herbage under foot, and the
        pale green leaves of the trees prolific,
In the distance the flowing glaze, the breast of the
        river, with a wind-dapple here and there,
With ranging hills on the banks, with many a line
        against the sky, and shadows,
And the city at hand with dwellings so dense, and
        stacks of chimneys,
And all the scenes of life and the workshops, and
        the workmen homeward returning.

12

Lo, body and soul—this land,
My own Manhattan with spires, and the sparkling
        and hurrying tides, and the ships,
The varied and ample land, the South and the
        North in the light, Ohio's shores and
        flashing Missouri,

And ever the far-spreading prairies cover'd with
       grass and corn.

Lo, the most excellent sun so calm and haughty,
The violet and purple morn with just-felt breezes,
The gentle soft-born measureless light,
The miracle spreading bathing all, the fulfill'd noon,
The coming eve delicious, the welcome night and
       the stars,
Over my cities shining all, enveloping man and land.

13

Sing on, sing on you gray-brown bird,
Sing from the swamps, the recesses, pour your
       chant from the bushes,
Limitless out of the dusk, out of the cedars and
       pines.

Sing on dearest brother, warble your reedy song,
Loud human song, with voice of uttermost woe.

O liquid and free and tender!
O wild and loose to my soul—O wondrous singer!
You only I hear—yet the star holds me, (but will
       soon depart,)
Yet the lilac with mastering odor holds me.

14

Now while I sat in the day and look'd forth,
In the close of the day with its light and the fields
       of spring, and the farmers preparing their
       crops,
In the large unconscious scenery of my land with
       its lakes and forests,
In the heavenly aerial beauty, (after the perturb'd
       winds and the storms,)
Under the arching heavens of the afternoon swift
       passing, and the voices of children and
       women,
The many-moving sea-tides, and I saw the ships
       how they sail'd,
And the summer approaching with richness, and
       the fields all busy with labor,
And the infinite separate houses, how they all
       went on, each with its meals and minutia
       of daily usages,
And the streets how their throbbings throbb'd, and
       the cities pent—lo, then and there,
Falling upon them all and among them all,
       enveloping me with the rest,
Appear'd the cloud, appear'd the long black trail,
And I knew death, its thought, and the sacred
       knowledge of death.

Then with the knowledge of death as walking one
       side of me,

And the thought of death close-walking the other
        side of me,
And I in the middle as with companions, and as
        holding the hands of companions,
I fled forth to the hiding receiving night that talks
        not,
Down to the shores of the water, the path by the
        swamp in the dimness,
To the solemn shadowy cedars and ghostly pines
        so still.

And the singer so shy to the rest receiv'd me,
The gray-brown bird I know receiv'd us comrades
        three,
And he sang the carol of death, and a verse for
        him I love.

From deep secluded recesses,
From the fragrant cedars and the ghostly pines so
        still,
Came the carol of the bird.

And the charm of the carol rapt me
As I held as if by their hands my comrades in the
        night,
And the voice of my spirit tallied the song of the
        bird.

Come lovely and soothing death,
Undulate round the world, serenely arriving, arriving,

In the day, in the night, to all, to each,
Sooner or later delicate death.

Prais'd be the fathomless universe,
For life and joy, and for objects and knowledge curious,
And for love, sweet love—but praise! praise! praise!
For the sure-enwinding arms of cool-enfolding death.

Dark mother always gliding near with soft feet,
Have none chanted for thee a chant of fullest welcome?
Then I chant it for thee, I glorify thee above all,
I bring thee a song that when thou must indeed come,
          come unfalteringly.

Approach strong deliveress,
When it is so, when thou hast taken them I joyously
          sing the dead,
Lost in the loving floating ocean of thee,
Laved in the flood of thy bliss O death.

From me to thee glad serenades,
Dances for thee I propose saluting thee, adornments
          and feastings for thee,
And the sights of the open landscape and the high-
          spread sky are fitting,
And life and the fields, and the huge and thoughtful
          night.

The night in silence under many a star,
The ocean shore and the husky whispering wave whose
    voice I know,
And the soul turning to thee O vast and well-veil'd
    death,
And the body gratefully nestling close to thee.

Over the tree-tops I float thee a song,
Over the rising and sinking waves, over the myriad
    fields and the prairies wide,
Over the dense-pack'd cities all and the teeming
    wharves and ways,
I float this carol with joy, with joy to thee O death.

15

To the tally of my soul,
Loud and strong kept up the gray-brown bird,
With pure deliberate notes spreading filling the
    night.

Loud in the pines and cedars dim,
Clear in the freshness moist and the swamp-
    perfume,
And I with my comrades there in the night.

While my sight that was bound in my eyes unclosed,
As to long panoramas of visions.

And I saw askant the armies,
I saw as in noiseless dreams hundreds of battle-flags,

Borne through the smoke of the battles and pierc'd
      with missiles I saw them,
And carried hither and yon through the smoke,
      and torn and bloody,
And at last but a few shreds left on the staffs, (and
      all in silence,)
And the staffs all splinter'd and broken.

I saw battle-corpses, myriads of them,
And the white skeletons of young men, I saw them,
I saw the debris and debris of all the slain soldiers
      of the war,
But I saw they were not as was thought,
They themselves were fully at rest, they suffer'd not,
The living remain'd and suffer'd, the mother suffer'd,
And the wife and the child and the musing
      comrade suffer'd,
And the armies that remain'd suffer'd.

16

Passing the visions, passing the night,
Passing, unloosing the hold of my comrades' hands,
Passing the song of the hermit bird and the
      tallying song of my soul,
Victorious song, death's outlet song, yet varying
      ever-altering song,
As low and wailing, yet clear the notes, rising and
      falling, flooding the night,
Sadly sinking and fainting, as warning and
      warning, and yet again bursting with joy,

Covering the earth and filling the spread of the
        heaven,
As that powerful psalm in the night I heard from
        recesses,
Passing, I leave thee lilac with heart-shaped leaves,
I leave thee there in the door-yard, blooming,
        returning with spring.
I cease from my song for thee,
From my gaze on thee in the west, fronting the
        west, communing with thee,
O comrade lustrous with silver face in the night.

Yet each to keep and all, retrievements out of the
        night,
The song, the wondrous chant of the gray-brown
        bird,
And the tallying chant, the echo arous'd in my soul,
With the lustrous and drooping star with the
        countenance full of woe,
With the holders holding my hand nearing the call
        of the bird,
Comrades mine and I in the midst, and their
        memory ever to keep, for the dead I loved
        so well,
For the sweetest, wisest soul of all my days and
        lands—and this for his dear sake,
Lilac and star and bird twined with the chant of
        my soul,
There in the fragrant pines and the cedars dusk
        and dim.

O Captain! My Captain!

O Captain! my Captain! our fearful trip is done,
The ship has weather'd every rack, the prize we
      sought is won,
The port is near, the bells I hear, the people all
      exulting,
While follow eyes the steady keel, the vessel grim
      and daring;
      But O heart! heart! heart!
        O the bleeding drops of red,
          Where on the deck my Captain lies,
          Fallen cold and dead.

O Captain! my Captain! rise up and hear the bells;
Rise up—for you the flag is flung—for you the
      bugle trills,
For you bouquets and ribbon'd wreaths—for you
      the shores a-crowding,
For you they call, the swaying mass, their eager
      faces turning;
      Here Captain! dear father!
        This arm beneath your head!
          It is some dream that on the deck,
          You've fallen cold and dead.

My Captain does not answer, his lips are pale and
      still,
My father does not feel my arm, he has no pulse
      nor will,

The ship is anchor'd safe and sound, its voyage
            closed and done,
From fearful trip the victor ship comes in with
            object won;
            Exult O shores, and ring O bells!
            But I with mournful tread,
                Walk the deck my Captain lies,
                Fallen cold and dead.

Old Ireland

Far hence amid an isle of wondrous beauty,
Crouching over a grave an ancient sorrowful mother,
Once a queen, now lean and tatter'd seated on the
  ground,
Her old white hair drooping dishevel'd round her
  shoulders,
At her feet fallen an unused royal harp,
Long silent, she too long silent, mourning her
  shrouded hope and heir,
Of all the earth her heart most full of sorrow
  because most full of love.

Yet a word ancient mother,
You need crouch there no longer on the cold
  ground with forehead between your knees,
O you need not sit there veil'd in your old white
  hair so dishevel'd,
For know you the one you mourn is not in that
  grave,
It was an illusion, the son you love was not really
  dead,
The Lord is not dead, he is risen again young and
  strong in another country,
Even while you wept there by your fallen harp by
  the grave,

What you wept for was translated, pass'd from the
          grave,
The winds favor'd and the sea sail'd it,
And now with rosy and new blood,
Moves to-day in a new country.

Song at Sunset

Splendor of ended day floating and filling me,
Hour prophetic, hour resuming the past,
Inflating my throat, you divine average,
You earth and life till the last ray gleams I sing.

Open mouth of my soul uttering gladness,
Eyes of my soul seeing perfection,
Natural life of me faithfully praising things,
Corroborating forever the triumph of things.

Illustrious every one!
Illustrious what we name space, sphere of
        unnumber'd spirits,
Illustrious the mystery of motion in all beings,
        even the tiniest insect,
Illustrious the attribute of speech, the senses, the
        body,
Illustrious the passing light—illustrious the pale
        reflection on the new moon in the western
        sky,
Illustrious whatever I see or hear or touch, to the
        last.

Good in all,
In the satisfaction and aplomb of animals,
In the annual return of the seasons,
In the hilarity of youth,
In the strength and flush of manhood,

In the grandeur and exquisiteness of old age,
In the superb vistas of death.

Wonderful to depart!
Wonderful to be here!
The heart, to jet the all-alike and innocent blood!
To breathe the air, how delicious!
To speak—to walk—to seize something by the
        hand!
To prepare for sleep, for bed, to look on my rose-
        color'd flesh!
To be conscious of my body, so satisfied, so large!
To be this incredible God I am!
To have gone forth among other Gods, these men
        and women I love.

Wonderful how I celebrate you and myself!
How my thoughts play subtly at the spectacles
        around!
How the clouds pass silently overhead!
How the earth darts on and on! and how the sun,
        moon, stars, dart on and on!
How the water sports and sings! (surely it is alive!)
How the trees rise and stand up, with strong
        trunks, with branches and leaves!
(Surely there is something more in each of the
        tree, some living soul.)

O amazement of things—even the least particle!
O spirituality of things!

O strain musical flowing through ages and
        continents, now reaching me and America!
I take your strong chords, I intersperse them, and
        cheerfully pass them forward.

I too carol the sun, usher'd or at noon, or as now,
        setting,
I too throb to the brain and beauty of the earth
        and of all the growths of the earth,
I too have felt the resistless call of myself.

As I steam'd down the Mississippi,
As I wander'd over the prairies,
As I have lived, as I have look'd through my
        windows my eyes,
As I went forth in the morning, as I beheld the
        light breaking in the east,
As I bathed on the beach of the Eastern Sea, and
        again on the beach of the Western Sea,
As I roam'd the streets of inland Chicago, whatever
        streets I have roam'd,
Or cities or silent woods, or even amid the sights
        of war,
Wherever I have been, I have charged myself with
        contentment and triumph.

I sing to the last the equalities modern or old,
I sing the endless finalés of things,
I say Nature continues, glory continues,
I praise with electric voice,

For I do not see one imperfection in the universe,
And I do not see one cause or result lamentable at
       last in the universe.

O setting sun! though the time has come,
I still warble under you, if none else does,
       unmitigated adoration.